Creative Serging Illustrated

The Complete Handbook for Decorative Overlock Sewing

Pati Palmer • Gail Brown • Sue Green

Chilton Book Company · Radnor, Pennsylvania

We could not have written this book without the gracious cooperation of representatives from many sewing machine companies. Our special thanks are extended to the following companies, listed in alphabetical order by the serger brand name: Baby Lock, Baby Lock, U.S.A., P.O. Box 2634, St. Louis, MO 63116; Bernette, Swiss Bernina Inc., 534 W. Chestnut, Hinsdale, IL 60521; Brother Lock, Brother International Corp., 8 Corporate Place, Piscataway, NJ 08854; Combi 10, Designer Lock and Janome Lock, New Home Sewing Machine Co., 171 Commerce Road, Carlstadt, NJ 07072; Consew and Tuffy Lock, Consolidated Sewing Machine Corp., 56-65 Rust Street, Maspeth, NY 11378; Elna Lock, Elna Inc., 7642 Washington Ave., S. Minneapolis, MN 55344; Handy Lock, Viking Distributing Co., 685 Market, Medford, OR 97504; Hobbylock, Pfaff American Sales Corp., 610 Winters Ave., Paramus, NJ 07652; Huskylock, Husqvarna Sewing Machine Co., Inc., 2300 Louisiana Ave., N. Minneapolis, MN 55427; Juki Lock, Juki Industries of America, Inc., 421 N. Midland Ave., Saddle Brook, NJ 07662; Mammy Lock, Brewer Sewing Supplies, 3800 West 42nd St., Chicago, IL 60632; Mini Lock, King Distributions, Inc., 599 Industrial Ave., Paramus, NJ 07652; National, Allied National, Inc., 13270 Capitol Ave., Oak Park, MI 48237; Necci Lock, Necchi Sewing Machines, U.S.A., Division of Allyn International Corp., 1075 Santa Fe Drive, Denver, CO 80204; Riccar Lock, Riccar America Company, 14281 Franklin Ave., Tustin, CA 92680; Simplicity Easy Lock, Tacony Corporation, P.O. Box 730, Fenton, MO 63026; Super Lock, The Viking-White Sewing Machine Co., 11750 Berea Road, Cleveland, OH 44111; Ultralock and The Singer Professional, The Singer Company, 135 Raritan Center Parkway, Edison, NJ 08818.

In addition, we would like to thank: Coats & Clark Inc.; Swiss-Metrosene, Inc.; Y.L.I. Corp.; McCall Pattern Company; Marta Alto, Naomi Baker, Lynette Black, Karen Dillon, Ann Price, Susan Pletsch, Lynn Raasch, Barbara Weiland O'Connell and Leslie Wood of Palmer/Pletsch Associates; and Bobbi Keeney, who remains our most proficient typist. Also, we thank Thelma Watson and Hazel Jens, avid home sewers who read our book for clarity; Ron Ellwanger, Jeff Watson and Jack Watson for putting up with us through the writing of this book. And to Pati's patient new daughter Melissa, born during the writing of this book!

ISBN 0-8019-7744-4

Photography by Larry Brazil; cover design by Kevin Culver, Culver Graphics; models: Sonya Gumm, Valerie Bolch, Olof Run Skuladottir, Hjordis Hugrun Sigurdardottir; photographed at the Alberta Humphreys estate; samples and clothing coordinated by Naomi Baker

Palmer/Pletsch Creative Serging edition design & production by Wisner Associates, Eugene, Oregon; technical and fashion illustrations by Kate Pryka; divider page fashion illustrations by Maggie Raguse

10 11 12 13 14   4 3 2 1 0 9

Contents

A Message from Robbie Fanning

The best books are those where you have a silent conversation with the author: "That's a good idea!" you say, or "how clever!" I've been having conversations with Pati Palmer's books for years. I know when a Palmer/Pletsch book arrives in my local sewing store that it will contain solid, up-to-date information with clear drawings and a sense of humor. The authors will have figured out the fastest, cleverest way to fit pants, tailor blazers, sew silk and Ultrasuede, plan my wedding and my wardrobe, and learn how to use my new serger. I buy every new Palmer/Pletsch book as it appears, knowing without even reading that it will be a valuable addition to my sewing library.

Therefore, when Chilton and I began to develop our Creative Machine Arts series, I contacted Pati. She and Gail Brown had already published Sewing With Sergers, an excellent beginning guide to sergers.

A confession: when it comes to my serger, I have been like a hesitant beginning sewer. I'd eye all the threads and tension dials suspiciously, as if they were there to thwart me. I'd panic at any unusual clunk and, above all, would never unthread the machine. For a year, I used my machine only for straightforward seams, nothing fancy. The thought of twirling tension dials or putting pearl cotton through loopers seemed too exotic, too much trouble—and besides, horrors!, I'd have to rethread the machine.

Though I had an owner's manual for my machine, I never "found the time" to explore rolled hems, flatlocking, or anything creative—but I didn't like this uneasy feeling. I prefer the attitude I have toward my sewing machine: pure unadulterated love. I take my sewing machine apart in a second; understand its innards and eccentricities; effortlessly change needles and thread, tensions and settings.

So I had an ulterior motive when I contacted Pati Palmer for this book.

I said (thinking of myself), "Once someone reads your book and learns how to use her serger, she'll want to apply her knowledge.

Will you write Son of Serger for our series?" I wanted a book with all the solid information of their other books, but in a slightly larger format, with the addition of color and black-and-white photos. Most of all, I wanted a book that would kick me into high gear on my serger, make me start twirling dials like a pro.

Pati, Gail, and Sue Green had already planned such a second serger book in Pati's usual small paperback format, but we all decided that there was merit in publishing both Palmer/Pletsch's version and Chilton's larger version.

We call ours Creative Serging Illustrated for several reasons. First, on our color pages you can see some of the exciting clothing possible with the serger. Secondly, we've added a photo section of the top-of-the-line sergers from the major manufacturers. Now you can survey the gamut of machines available to you. Third, we added a chapter called "The Serger Challenge," with ideas to encourage your creative imagination. And, finally, we've designed four exercises where you can practice what you've learned, manipulating stitch length, width, tension, and threads.

And me? Working on this book inspired me to learn to love my serger. I did the exercises, which made me feel comfortable about playing with my machine. I threaded and unthreaded with no second thoughts. I even worked through my (poorly written) owner's manual, constantly consulting this book to clear up misunderstandings. Then, by pinning my samples in this book, I truly had a creative serging illustrated book. So will you.

Robbie Fanning

Series Editor, Creative Machine Arts,
and co-author,
The Complete Book of Machine Embroidery

7

Introduction to Creative Serging

1• *Introduction to Creative Serging*

Creativity means originality, expressiveness and imagination. Sergers give us decorative possibilities that open a whole new world of creativity for the home sewer . . . a creativity that looks sophisticated, not cutesy!

A serger trims, then totally encases, an edge of fabric — unlike the zigzag on a conventional sewing machine. Also, since the stitches are formed over a metal stitch finger, the edge will never draw up, even on lightweight silkies. Because sergers have "loopers" that go **over** and **under** the fabric, heavy decorative threads, yarns, and ribbons can be used. These cannot be used on conventional machines because they will neither fit through the needle nor penetrate many fabrics.

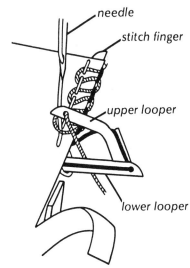

needle

stitch finger

upper looper

lower looper

WHAT IS DECORATIVE SERGING?

Whenever serging shows, it is decorative . . . even when using regular thread. Serging will show **more** if you shorten the stitch length, use a contrasting color thread, a heavier thread, or a shinier thread like silk, rayon, or metallic. The following are decorative uses of a serger:

• Exposed seams

• Satin stitched seam allowances that look like they are bound

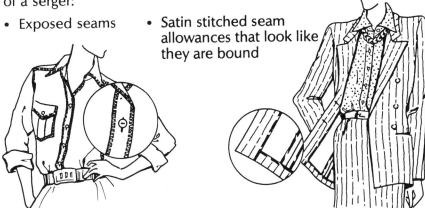

• Edges finished with a wide stitch

• Rolled edges serged with matching or contrasting thread

• Flatlocked seams

• Heirloom sewing with laces and trims attached with serging

Our first book, **Sewing With Sergers,** covered serger basics. Since then, we've learned a lot more about the use of decorative threads and creative uses of a serger. We will help you be adventurous and experiment with many different ideas. Also, we can now help you **solve** nearly **every problem** you might encounter on your serger. Thanks to our four-day Palmer/Pletsch Serger Workshops held in Portland, Oregon, we've learned a lot!

SERGERS HAVE IMPROVED

During the past twenty years, 1.4 million sergers have been manufactured in Japan and sold to home sewers in this country. Yet, ten years ago, only about 20,000 sergers were imported into the U.S. In 1986, over 600,000 were imported. With this increase in sales has come technological improvements. Serger manufacturers have added built-in lights, dials for adjusting stitch width and length, color-coded thread guides, markings on tension dials, more stitches, and improved instruction books. All of these contribute to our ability to use sergers creatively.

If you are one of those early birds who has already bought a serger, keep your first one even if you decide to upgrade. Today's luxury is having **TWO** sergers, like **TWO** cars! Keep one set up for regular seaming and one for a rolled edge.

MAKE YOUR FIRST DECORATIVE PROJECT EASY

For your first creative venture, choose one of the lighter weight decorative threads such as topstitching thread or Woolly Nylon and an easy-to-sew inexpensive fabric such as polar fleece or sweatshirting. For ideas, see our chapter on decorative sweatshirts.

The most important guideline for decorative serging is to **TEST** using a scrap of your garment fabric on the same grain. By adjusting the tension dials just a little, you can totally change the stitch or create a new one.

Child's decorative polar fleece coat

A creative sweatshirt

Once you've mastered decorative serging basics, graduate to heavier threads, yarns, and ribbons. Use this book to hold your hand as your become ULTRA CREATIVE. You won't believe how much fun you will have!

2 · *Serger Basics*

The serger, also called an overlock machine, stitches, trims, and overcasts in one step at almost twice the speed of a conventional sewing machine. A conventional sewing machine sews from 700 to 1100 stitches per minute and a serger sews up to 1700 stitches per minute.

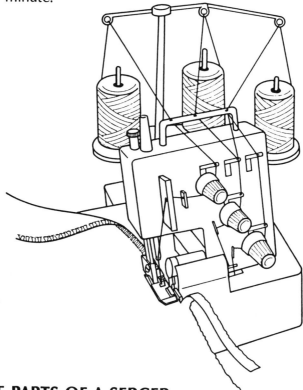

THE PARTS OF A SERGER

One important part of a serger not illustrated in our first book is what Sue lovingly calls "George". George is the extension on the back of the presser foot. Always put your threads **under** George before beginning to serge!

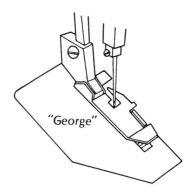

"George"

A 5-thread serger is illustrated here so that you can see the parts of a machine that has the maximum number of loopers and needles. For a 4-thread machine, just eliminate the left lower looper. For a 3-thread machine eliminate one needle as well. On a 2-thread machine, there is only one needle and one looper.

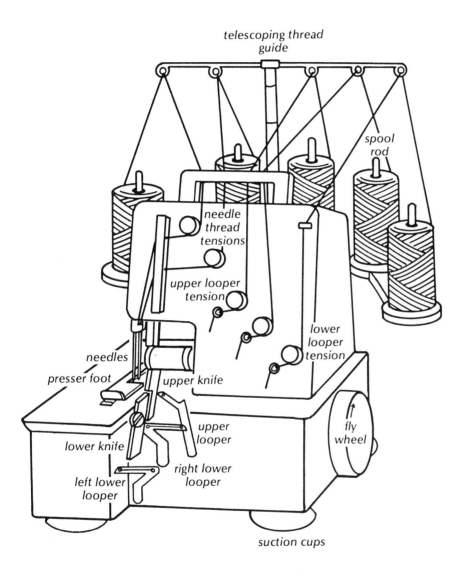

telescoping thread guide

spool rod

needle thread tensions

upper looper tension

lower looper tension

needles

presser foot

upper knife

lower knife

upper looper

left lower looper

right lower looper

fly wheel

suction cups

HOW ARE STITCHES FORMED ON SERGERS?

Stitch Name	How the Stitch is Formed

2-Thread Overedge

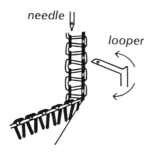

The looper goes over the top of the fabric, leaving a loop that is caught by the needle thread. Then the looper goes under the fabric, picks up the needle thread and pulls it to the edge of the fabric.

3-Thread Overlock

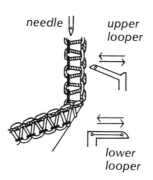

The upper looper goes over the top of the fabric, where it is caught by the needle thread and then it is caught by the lower looper on the edge.

The lower looper goes under the fabric and is caught by the needle thread and then goes out to the edge of the fabric where it is caught by the upper looper.

3/4-Thread Overlock
(A 3-thread overlock + an extra stitch down the middle. Two types are available.)

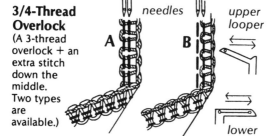

This is a 3-thread stitch with an extra needle thread. In "A" leave out left needle for a narrow or right needle for a wide 3-thread stitch. In "B" leave out the left needle for a narrow 3-thread stitch.

All 3/4-thread machines will make a 3-thread stitch alone. It is changed **only** by eliminating a needle. Width control is not infinite. However, an advantage is very wide stitch width.

- Called an "overedge" stitch because the threads do not connect or "lock" at the seamline; therefore, it is not used to sew seams.

NOTE: One manufacturer has invented the term "**seamlock**" for a 2-thread **seam**. A strong seam can be sewn by tightening the needle tension all the way and loosening the looper tension. The needle thread then forms a straight line and the looper wraps the edge.

- Perfect if you primarily want to finish seam allowances and edges.
- With only two threads, seam and edge finishes are less bulky — nice for lightweight fabrics or when using heavier decorative threads.
- Flatlocking is easy and very flat with a 2-thread stitch (see page 66).
- Some 2-thread machines can be adjusted to sew a rolled edge.

NOTE: There are 2-thread machines, but some 3-thread and all true 4-thread (chainstitch) machines can convert to two threads.

- Called an "overlock" stitch because the threads connect or "lock" at the seamline. Can be used to sew seams.
- Produces a balanced stitch that looks the same on both sides . . . great for reversibles.
- With three threads, seam and edge finishes can be slightly bulkier than with two threads because of the additional thread.
- Has lots of give, so is excellent for knits.
- 3-thread machines can flatlock (see page 66).

NOTE: Some 3-thread machines can convert to two threads. Check your manual.

- Like a 3-thread stitch with the addition of an extra stitch down the middle for added durability.
- All four threads are not necessary for a serged seam.
- May serge with only three threads.
- Has as much give as a 3-thread stitch.
- Interesting decorative effects created when different color threads are used in the needles. 3/4-thread machines can flatlock, but one needle must be dropped.

NOTE: Several manufacturers are now introducing 3/4-thread machines that can also sew a 3-thread as well as a 2-thread stitch. We call them 2/3/4-thread machines.

Stitch Name	How the Stitch is Formed

True 4-Thread

(This means all **4** threads are needed to sew a serged **seam**.)

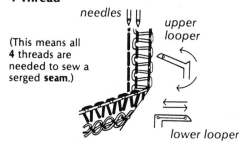

The left needle and the lower looper form a 2-thread chain stitch.

The right needle and the upper looper form the 2-thread overedge stitch described above.

5-Thread

These are so new that as we write this book, none are yet available. They will be able to sew a chain stitch with either a 2-thread overedge stitch or a 3-thread overlock stitch. Each stitch can also be sewn alone.

The chain combined with a 3-thread overlock:

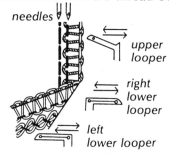

The chain — the left needle and left lower looper form a 2-thread chain stitch.

The 3-thread overlock — formed as described on page 14.

The chain combined with a 2-thread overedge:

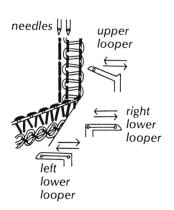

The chain — formed as described above.

The 2-thread overedge — thread only the right lower looper, not the upper looper. The upper looper has a hook which carries the right lower looper thread over the fabric to meet the needle thread. The two working together replace the "over/under" action of the upper looper on a 4/2-thread machine.

- Made up of a 2-thread chainstitch and a 2-thread overedge stitch. All four threads are necessary to sew a serged seam.
- Well-suited for ravelly, loosely woven fabrics because the chain forms a strong seam and the seam allowance is wider.
- The seam is also wide enough to press flat and even top-stitch.
- It has less stretch than a 3-thread stitch so can stabilize stretchy areas.
- Used whenever a wider seam allowance is desirable for strength (upholstery) or when seam needs to be pressed flat (jackets, slacks).
- Some 4/2-thread machines can sew a rolled edge.

NOTE: Dropping the left needle leaves a 2-thread overedge stitch for professional finishing of seam allowances and flatlocking. Dropping the right needle leaves the straight chain stitch.

- Sews a 2-thread chain stitch in combination with a 2-thread overedge **or** a 3-thread overlock stitch.

- Chain stitch, 2-thread overedge, or 3-thread overlock can each be used independently.

- By using the 2-thread chain stitch **and** 3-thread overlock stitch together, the seam is sewn twice for added durability.

- Use the 3-thread overlock stitch alone for seams that require stretch.

- Can sew rolled edge with either 2-thread or 3-thread stitch.

- A very wide 8.5mm seam width is created when the chain is sewn with either the 2- or 3-thread stitch. Great for durability.

THE SERGER GALLERY

Here are the top-of-the-line serger models from the major companies, current at press time. Of course every company has many models of sergers, from two-thread machines up, and the field is developing fast, but this will introduce you to what's available.

Bernette 335 (Bernina)

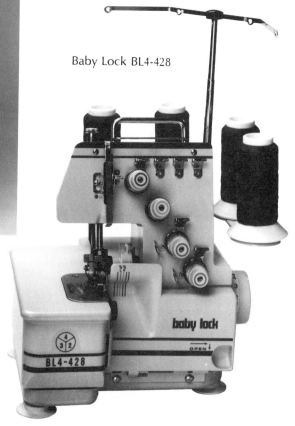

Baby Lock BL4-428

Hobbylock 794 (Pfaff)

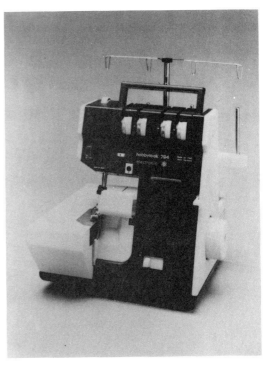

Brother Lock 526-D

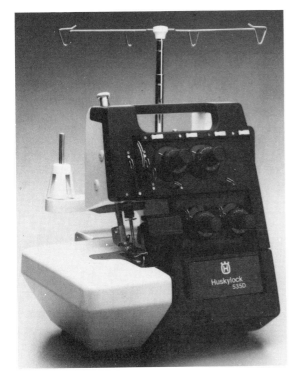

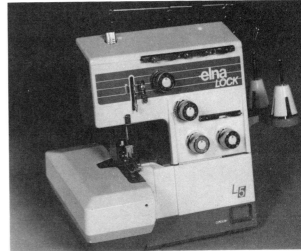

Elna Lock L5

Huskylock 535D
(Viking White)

New Home
Lock 777

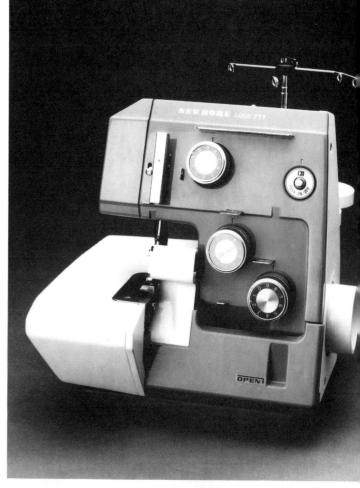

Mini Lock FR-855L

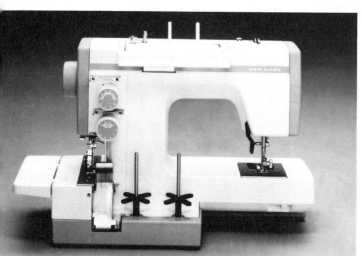

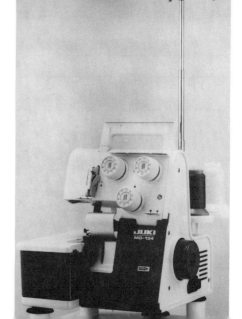

New Home Combi DX

Juki MO-134

Riccar Lock RL-343DR

Simplicity Easy Lock 880

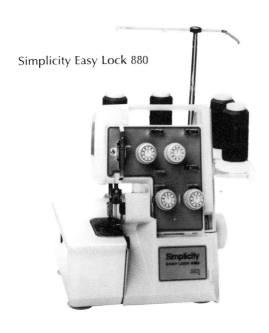

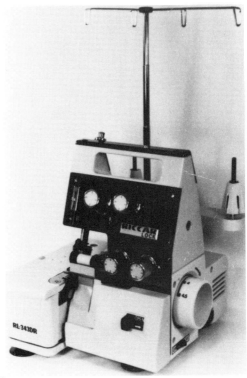

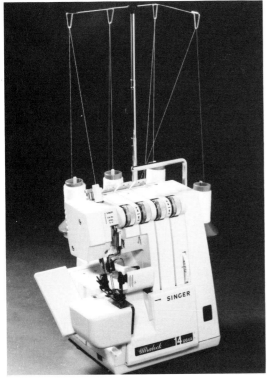

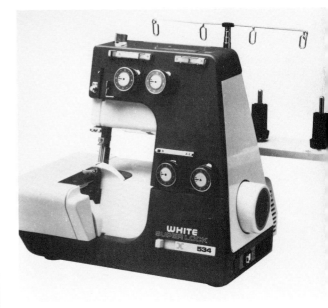

White Superlock 534

Ultralock 14 U64A (Singer)

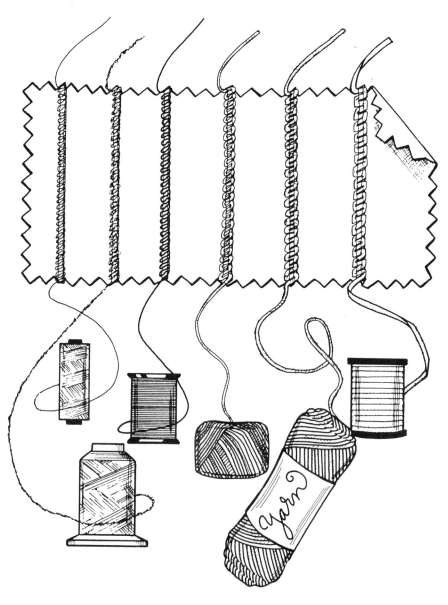

Decorative Thread Glossary

CHAPTER 3 · Decorative Thread Glossary

Use this chapter as a reference when choosing and serging with decorative threads, yarns, and ribbons. We've listed them in order of serging difficulty, starting with the easiest. At the end of the chapter we've summarized tension tips for each type in a handy quick-reference chart.

Regular Thread — Choose extra-fine, serger, or all-purpose thread. The latter is the heaviest, yet the difference is subtle. One advantage of using these three types of thread decoratively is that you can use them in the needle as well as the loopers. Also, all-purpose thread is available in a wide range of colors.

For better coverage, we recommend a short stitch length when using regular thread, especially on the edge of a woven fabric. We call a short stitch a "satin" stitch. With knits or non-wovens you can use a longer stitch length if a more open look is desired.

For conventional spools, use the cap that comes with your machine to help the thread reel off quickly and evenly. Place the cap on the spool or the rod. Check your manual. Place the notched side of the spool down.

notch

Creative Uses:

- Lapped seams and edges on a shirt
- Lightweight rolled edges on a scarf or full skirt hem
- Lapped seams on synthetic suede

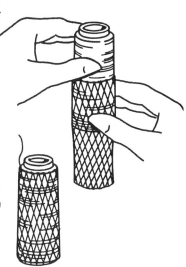

Nylon Filament Thread — Some ready-to-wear manufacturers use this translucent thread in their general sewing so they don't need to change thread every time they change fabric color. It automatically "matches" the fabric. Most of the newer nylon thread is soft and not wiry. It can be used in the needle as well as in both loopers. Tension settings are generally normal. You may need to cover the spool with netting to prevent spilling or slipping off the spool.

One of our favorite uses of nylon filament thread is in the needle and the **lower** looper. Use a heavy decorative thread, yarn, or ribbon in the **upper** looper. The "invisible" nylon makes the upper looper thread appear as if it is just floating on the surface of the fabric.

NOTE: A semi-transparent lightweight polyester thread is also available and comes in several colors. One is Metrolene by Mettler.

Topstitching Thread — A highly twisted, cord-like polyester or cotton-covered polyester thread in a buttonhole twist. It covers an edge better than regular thread and is available in many colors.

Topstitching thread can be used in the needles as well as the loopers. Use a spool cap because the thread tends to embed itself on the spool. The wide angle created by the spool cap (page 23) helps the thread flow freely.

We love topstitching thread, but we hope manufacturers will eventually put more than 50 yards on a spool. Before beginning, make sure you have enough thread to complete an entire edge. See page 35 for estimating yardage. If you do run short, see page 43 for repair tips. We suggest buying one spool **just for testing.**

Creative Uses:
- Flatlocked and fringed challis scarves
- Edges of coats and jackets that are serged rather than stitched and turned
- Wonderful for rolled edges on napkins as it washes well
- Decorative stitching on synthetic suedes and leathers
- Flatlocking on sweatshirts and actionwear (washes well)

Rayon Thread — Looks similar to silk with its beautiful sheen, but much less costly. Available in fine, medium, and heavy weights, the most prevalent is a weight about halfway between regular and topstitching thread.

Rayon thread is primarily used in the upper looper. It tends to break easily when used in the needle and lower looper due to friction. It also slips through the tension discs easily due to its slickness, so you may need to tighten the tensions slightly. Serge a test sample. For rolled edges use it only in the upper looper. The lower loop needs to be tightened a lot, difficult with thin slippery thread. It is available on cones and spools and may need netting to keep it from spilling.

Rayon thread comes in a wide range of very intense colors including variegated. Brands available include Madeira, Natesh, Sulky, and Y.L.I.

Creative Uses:

- Wide, shiny satin stitch on the edge of Chanel-style jackets (resembles trim)
- Rolled edges on scarves
- Medium width satin stitch in unlined jackets to resemble a silky Hong Kong seam finish
- Shiny rolled edge seams in heirloom sewing

Silk Thread — Similar to rayon only more costly and harder to find. Topstitching weight comes on spools with a small amount of yardage.

Woolly Nylon — In 1984, Y.L.I. introduced its Woolly Nylon to the homesewing market. It is a heat-set texturized or crimped thread that looks fuzzy like wool. It is about the same weight as regular sewing thread; however, because it is lofty and not twisted, it spreads to cover an edge. Similar products are Metroflock by Metrosene and S-T-R-E-T-C-H-Y by Belding Corticelli.

These threads can be used in the needle as well as the loopers. We find it necessary to loosen tensions considerably to allow it to flow without too much stretching. The inherent stretchiness actually "tightens up" the seam, making a **very strong** seam that won't pull apart — perfect for activewear.

Creative Uses:

- Edges of a single-layer wool cape (no facings and reversible)
- Edges of placemats — good "coverage", washable, and prevents corners from ravelling
- Seams in ravelly fabrics or activewear when strength is essential

Metallic Thread — There is a difference among brands. Some are very fine, resembling silk, while others are coarse and metal-like. Your choice depends on the look you want. Metallics work best in the upper looper. Some will strip back or fray when used in the needle or lower looper. Test first!

Use gold or gray regular thread in the needle to blend with gold or silver metallics. With a shorter stitch length, the coarser metallics lie at random. They don't look as smooth and even as the finer metallics. Try tightening the tensions slightly to smooth them out. Some may look better with a longer stitch length. They come on cones, tubes and spools.

Creative uses:

- Rolled edges on holiday napkins
- A wide satin stitch on edges of placemats
- The neckline of a sweaterknit using a wide width
- Pintucks on an evening blouse
- Ruffles on sheers
- Dancewear
- Fancy scarf edges
- Dramatic touch on a basic black or white dress

Crochet Thread — Available in cotton or acrylic fibers and in many colors. The cotton variety, a highly twisted mercerized thread, is slightly thicker than topstitching thread. It is strong and easy to use in upper as well as lower loopers, but too thick for the needle. The acrylic variety is similar to cotton only slightly fuzzier, hence a perfect coordinate for wools and sweater knits. Coats & Clark is a major manufacturer of these and their Knit-Cro-Sheen is available in both cotton and acrylic. Crochet thread is wound on balls that average 175 yards each. See pages 35 and 40 for hand feeding and tension tips.

Creative uses:

- Gail sewed a single layer jacket without facings using upholstery fabric. She used acrylic crochet thread in both loopers to finish the outside edges, making the jacket reversible
- Edges of quilted placemats
- Edges of thick fuzzy woolens to create your own blankets and throws

Pearl Cotton — A mercerized 100% cotton that is shiny, soft, and not highly twisted. Two widely distributed sizes are #8 (finer) and #5 (thicker). It is available in 50 yard balls or smaller 10 yard skeins. Its color range is broad and includes interesting variegated shades.

Our preference is to use pearl cotton in the upper looper. You **can** use it in the lower looper, but the extra thread guides can cause fraying. Also, because of the loose twist, the needle can catch the pearl cotton as it is "thrown" over the top of the fabric by the upper looper. Serging slowly will generally solve this problem. Like crochet thread, pearl cotton is sold in balls. See pages 35 and 40 for hand feeding and tension tips.

Creative Uses:

- Flatlocked fringe on a wool challis scarf

- Edges of a cotton interlock knit in a sporty jumpsuit using a bright contrast color

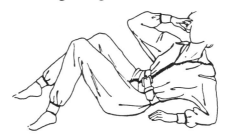

- Edges of baby clothes and receiving blankets using a variegated pastel color

Yarn — The key to successfully serging with yarn is to use one that is fine, strong, tightly twisted, and smooth. To test for adequate strength, pull on a strand. If it breaks easily, it will also break easily when serging. If too loosely twisted, it can be caught by the needle and jam your machine. If lumpy, it won't flow evenly through the tension guides.

Easy to use — a fine, even, tightly twisted yarn.

Difficult to use — a thick, slubby, untwisted yarn.

We've had good luck with baby yarn (comes in pastel and variegated shades), as well as sock or sweater yarn (comes in neutral colors). Both are fine, strong and twisted enough for smooth feeding. Sport or "fingering" weight yarns are available in a wider color range, but each brand and fiber varies, so test serge on scraps **first**.

Keep fiber content in mind too. Acrylic yarn works well as it is quite strong. Wool yarn is weaker, but twisting the plies can add strength. Blending wool with nylon also helps. You may try cotton and silk yarns; however, we've found that they can lack the resiliency and drape necessary for hiccup-free serging.

Yarn is generally used in the upper looper only. The extra thread guides in the lower looper can cause fraying. See pages 35 and 40 for feeding and tension tips.

Creative Ideas

- Variegated pastel yarn on edges of a double-layer receiving blanket.

- Edges of a boiled wool jacket

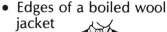

- Edges of a single-layer wool cape

- Neckline, sleeve, and bottom edges of a sweater

Ribbon — Soft knitting ribbon 1/6" to 1/4" wide works well in the upper looper of a three-thread and the looper of a two-thread serger. See pages 35 and 40 for feeding and tension tips. Y.L.I. is one of the major distributors of decorative knitting ribbons. The following are available.

Silk Ribbon — Expensive, but can be purchased by the yard, rather than by the spool. See page 35 for estimating yardage.

Acrylic Ribbon — Very shiny, drapable, and soft like silk, but less expensive. Often called synthetic silk. Another suitable silk substitute is rayon, but may, however, break more than the acrylic silk-likes.

Cotton Ribbon — Durable and washable. Great as a trim for children's clothes. Choose a very fine, soft type for easiest sewing.

Polyester Ribbon — Generally too stiff, but worth a test.

Creative Ideas:

- Edges of ruffles for childrenswear and frou-frou blouses
- Edges of sweaterknits . . . the combination of textures is lovely
- As part of an heirloom serging scheme, add a row or two of ribbon serging

DECORATIVE THREAD, YARN, AND RIBBON GUIDE

The next chapter goes into detail on handling decorative thread, yarn, and ribbon; however, use this handy chart for quick reference.

Thread	Needle(s)	Upper Looper	Lower Looper	Tension
Clear Nylon	Yes	Yes	Yes	Normal
Topstitching	Yes	Yes	Yes	Slightly Looser
Rayon	Can Break	Yes	Can Break	Tighten
Woolly Nylon	Yes	Yes	Yes	Loosen
Metallic	May Fray	Yes	May Fray	Normal, Test
Crochet	Too Thick	Yes	Sometimes	Loosen a Lot
Pearl Cotton	Too Thick	Yes	Sometimes	May need to loosen or remove completely from tension disc and/or thread guides.
Yarn	Too Thick	Yes	Sometimes	
Ribbon (silky)	Too Thick	Yes	Sometimes	

CREATIVE SERGING *ILLUSTRATED*:
KNOW YOUR THREADS

One of the best gifts you can give yourself is a record of *your* threads worked in *your* machine. Below are instructions for creating a sampler of threads, which you can pin to this page or keep in a separate notebook. Use the chart on the previous page for suggested tension settings. Since this exercise requires you to set up your machine with heavier thread than you may be accustomed to, you may want to wait until you've read through the next chapter before making the sample.

1. Collect a range of threads, from lightweight sewing to heavy-weight crochet cotton. Arrange them in order of thickness.

2. Cut two pieces of sturdy fabric (wool, jacket-weight fabric, etc.), each about 12" x 30". Mark vertical lines every 1-1/2". One piece will be for practice and one for your permanent record.

3. Set up your machine for regular seams. Plan to try the lighter weight threads first. As you experiment with heavier threads, you will need to lengthen the stitch.

4. Fold the experimental material wrong sides together on the left vertical line and serge down the fold, barely cutting off the fold. Stop serging about every 5" and check for proper tension settings. Make adjustments. When you are pleased, fold the permanent record on the left vertical line. Make a permanent record of that thread. Write the settings you used below.

5. Continue experimenting with increasingly heavy threads and recording the results. Now you really know your threads!

		TENSIONS					
		NEEDLE(S)		LOOPER(S)		STITCH	
NOTES:	THREAD	LN	RN	UL	LL	Length	Width

(l to r) Know Your Threads: regular, topstitching, rayon, silk, woolly nylon, me-tallic, crochet, pearl cotton, yarn, ribbon

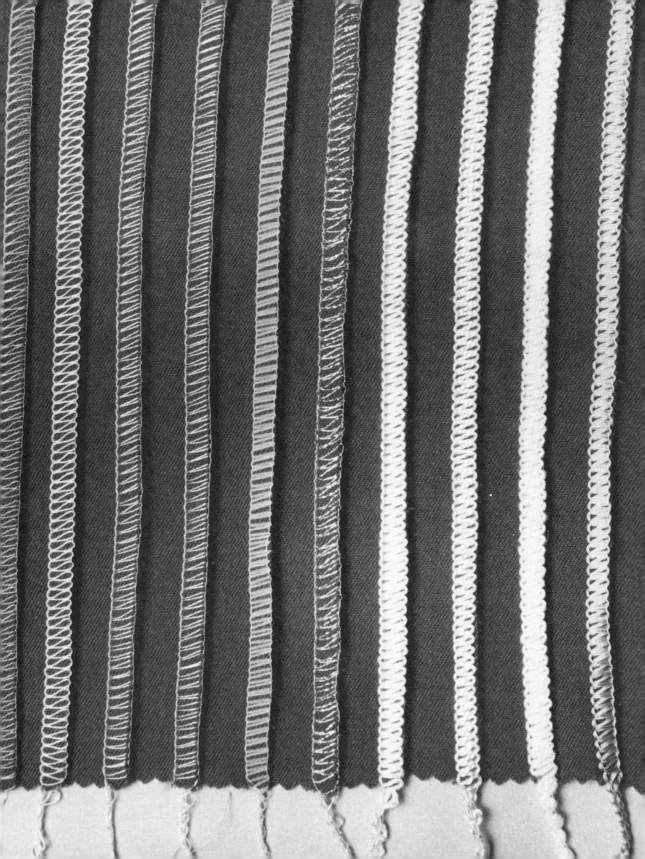

(Overleaf left and above) To accent this double-sided upholstery fabric, the jacket was made single layer (see Chapter 7 for Gail's Five-Step Jacket). Seams, edges, and hems were finished with a wide three-thread stitch, using acrylic crochet thread in the upper and lower loopers and serger thread in the needle. Gail had a friend knit the sweater yardage by machine, stabilized it with fusible tricot, then cut the top out, finishing the edges with the same stitch and thread used on the jacket. See Chapter 13.

The sweater applique, which Naomi Baker cut from the linen-look skirt fabric, was finished with satin stitching on a conventional sewing machine. Then she straight stitched it to the sweaterknit yardage top. Sweater edges were finished with a wide two-thread overedge, with yarn in the looper.

Variegated crochet cotton was used in the upper looper of a wide, close three-thread stitch to finish the edges of these mother-daughter outfits. Courtesy of "Sewing Today Across the USA" fashion shows.

CHAPTER 4 • *Decorative Basics*

Read this chapter before you begin decorative serging and you will avoid lots of frustration. Decorative serging is very creative, but you are pushing your serger to do more than its basic functions. With patience, you will be able to create looks you've never before thought possible. You'll really have a one-of-a-kind garment!

WHERE TO USE DECORATIVE THREADS ON YOUR SERGER

Generally, we use heavier decorative threads in the **upper looper**. There are fewer thread guides, so less stress is exerted on the thread. The lower looper has two holes and more thread guides causing stress and thread breakage.

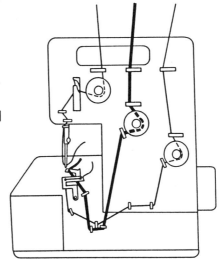

Lighter weight decorative threads can be used anywhere, even in the needle. Make sure the needle is large enough to accommodate the thread, yet not so large it damages the fabric. We use a size 14 for topstitching thread and an 11 or 12 for regular thread.

THREADING TIPS

- **Thread in proper order** — Check your manual for recommended order. In our first book we started with the lower looper, but since the upper looper thread guides are usually **behind** the lower looper thread guides, it may be easier to begin with the upper looper, then thread the lower looper and finally the needle.

- **All guides must be threaded!** — Missing a guide is the number one cause of stitching problems on a serger. Always DOUBLE CHECK the guides.

- **Make sure the looper threads aren't tangled or they will break!**

Good	**Good**	**Disaster**
Totally separate	Lower looper thread over upper looper thread	Lower looper thread between upper looper and upper looper thread

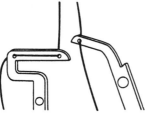  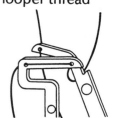

- **Don't use too heavy thread, yarn, or ribbon** — As a rule of thumb, if you have to **force** a double layer of decorative thread through the looper, it is **too** heavy to use on your machine.

- **There is an easy way to get a heavy thread through a small hole** — You can bend or break the looper threader that comes with some machines if you use it with heavy threads.

Instead, form a thread "cradle". Cut twelve inches of regular thread and wrap it around your heavier thread forming a loop. Then thread **both** ends of the regular thread through the looper hole. Use tweezers if necessary. Pull the heavier thread through the hole.

- **Be sure threads are engaged in tension discs** — Tug on threads just above and below the tension discs to make sure they are engaged. You should feel resistance on each thread.

- **After threading, "clear" threads before beginning to stitch** —

If you turn the flywheel around while threading, the needle thread will wrap around the lower looper causing breakage.

To prevent this problem, slide a seam ripper or similar tool under presser foot to draw up needle thread.

HOW MUCH DECORATIVE THREAD WILL I NEED?

It is frustrating to run out of thread. To estimate what is needed, Sue serged one yard of fabric with five types of decorative threads, yarns, and ribbons. Then she measured the amount used. Her stitch length was 2.5mm and width 5.0mm. She found the following:

Thread	Yards per looper needed to sew one yard of fabric
Pearl cotton	6-1/2
Topstitching thread	7
Crochet thread	8
Sport yarn	5-1/2
1/8" ribbon	7-1/2

Add to these amounts one yard for threading the machine and at least six yards for testing. Of course, if you change your stitch length and width, the amounts given in the chart will vary.

You may wonder why more crochet thread is used than ribbon. Crochet thread is wiry and lies on the fabric in a neat rounded "S" pattern. Ribbon is softer and folds over on top of itself; therefore, less is used. Why is so much less yarn used? Yarn stretches or elongates as it goes through the machine.

REEL OFF BY HAND WHEN USING SKEINS OR BALLS

If your decorative thread, yarn, or ribbon is **not** wound on spools, you must make sure it **feeds freely** as you serge. Any restriction on the thread will cause uneven stitching.

At first, we rewound thread from balls and skeins onto an empty cone or spool, but we found it added tension to the thread. We now recommend placing the ball or skein on its side on the table next to the machine, in a bowl, or on the floor. Then reel off a large quantity and serge—reel and serge—reel and serge. Just don't forget to keep reeling so there is plenty of slack between the ball or skein and the first thread guide.

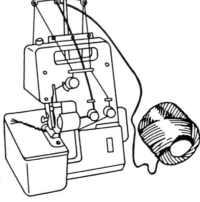

ALWAYS TEST FIRST!

It's difficult to correct a mistake. Pati learned the hard way. Her round-neck top grew into a "U"-neck style, because she forgot to test. After all, the **easiest** way to correct a problem is to cut away your mistake.

You will need 30" of fabric for thorough testing. Test on the same grain you'll be sewing. A **long** strip of fabric allows you to serge 5", stop and look at both sides, adjust tensions if necessary, and serge another 5". Do this until you achieve the look desired.

SEW SLOWLY

We can't emphasize enough the importance of sewing **slowly**. Even though your serger was made for speed, heavier threads pose a variety of potential problems. Also, if you serge too fast, extra tension will be placed on the thread and cause uneven stitching.

STITCH WIDTH

A wider stitch shows off the decorative thread better. We recommend beginning your TEST sample with the widest stitch and narrowing it a little at a time until you achieve the look you want.

STITCH LENGTH

Begin serging your TEST sample with the **longest** stitch possible to prevent jamming under the presser foot. Gradually work shorter until the desired look is achieved. Remember, "fatter" threads take up more room (as shown in our example) even though the stitch length is the same.

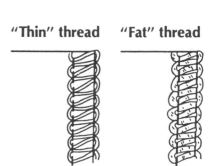

"Thin" thread   "Fat" thread

STEPS TO HEADACHE-FREE DECORATIVE SERGING

After threading the machine, use the following order for TEST sewing:

1. Set the stitch length and width according to the above instructions.

2. Rotate the handwheel by hand. See if the stitches are forming on the stitch finger.

3. It is not always necessary to lift presser foot during regular serging. However, you MUST LIFT the presser foot and place fabric under it when using decorative threads. It helps begin the "feeding" and prevents jamming.

4. Always at least **skim** the fabric edge with the knives for even width stitches, even if not trimming away any seam allowance.

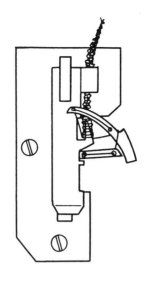

5. Begin sewing SLOWLY! Check your stitches every five inches.

YOUR THREAD BREAKS DURING TESTING

If one of your threads breaks during testing, try the following:

1. Double-check to see if the machine is threaded correctly.

2. Check to see if the threads are caught in the spool's notch.

3. Check to see if all threads are engaged in tension discs.

4. Try loosening the tension on the thread that broke.

5. If all else fails, re-thread the machine from scratch!

6. It still breaks? Re-thread the machine with regular thread in order to determine whether you have a mechanical problem or your machine just doesn't like that particular decorative thread.

EVERYTHING YOU EVER WANTED TO KNOW ABOUT TENSION

Every serger has tension dials. Sue prefers not to use this term. It reminds her of tension headaches! Instead, she calls them "stitch formers". And that is really what they are. Even a slight tension change can alter the look of the stitch. In decorative serging, there is no RIGHT or WRONG tension — whatever tension achieves the look desired is the correct tension.

NOTE: See our first book, **Sewing With Sergers**, for in-depth tension diagrams for all types of stitches.

Tension dials are mounted on the outside or set into the machine. Those that are numbered turn one to two rotations to loosen or tighten. Those not numbered can turn up to ten times. For these, turning two to three times may be required to make a slight change.

Gail's favorite way of remembering which way to turn the dial is a saying: "RIGHTY, TIGHTY and LEFTY, LOOSEY". Silly as it sounds, you won't forget it.

This doesn't always work for built-in dials. We suggest looking at your manual and putting arrows on your machine with masking tape for quick reference. Generally, the bigger the numbers, the tighter the tension.

WHICH DIAL
CONTROLS WHICH THREAD?

How about another rule? When there are four dials, the top two are for the needles and the lower two are for the loopers. The top left is for the left needle and the right for the right needle. If the two lower ones are at the same level, the one on the left is the upper looper and the one on the right is the lower looper. Mark them with masking tape until you can quickly remember their function.

left needle   right needle   upper looper   lower looper

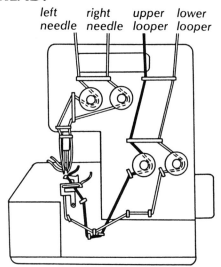

THE SECRET TO CORRECTING
TENSION PROBLEMS

Don't turn more than one dial at a time. Adjust the dial that appears too tight first, then TEST SEW. If the looper threads are unbalanced, do the same. Loosen the tight one first. If that doesn't solve the problem, return that dial to its original position and tighten the one that appears too loose. How do you know which is too tight? Read on . . .

HOW TO RECOGNIZE TENSION PROBLEMS

Diagnosis of tension problems is easy if you know what to look for. Remember the following:

1. The needle tension dial controls the **seamline**.

2. The upper looper tension dial controls the **top** side of the overcast.

3. The lower looper tension dial controls the **bottom** side of the overcast.

If your seam is pulling apart like this . . .

. . . tighten the needle tension.

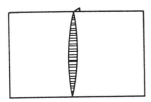

If your seam puckers like this . . .

. . . loosen the needle tension.

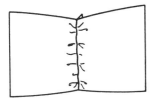

If your stitch looks like this, loosen the upper looper and/or tighten the lower looper.

If your stitch looks like this, tighten the upper looper and/or loosen the lower looper.

HEAVY DECORATIVE THREADS BREAK TENSION RULES

To get a **balanced** stitch, each tension dial will be set at a different place when using a thick thread in one looper and a thin thread in the other. You will need to ignore the recommended settings in your manual.

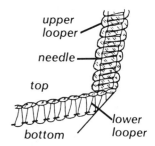

upper looper

needle

top

lower looper

bottom

The reason is that heavier threads create more **resistance** in the tension dials. A fatter thread simply **takes up more room**.

Decrease tension for thicker threads.

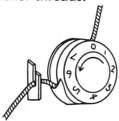

Increase tension for thinner threads.

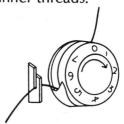

If you loosen the tension on heavy thread completely and it is still too tight, try removing the thread from one or more thread guides. If that doesn't work, completely remove the thread from the tension dial as shown. **Experiment!**

If your machine has a "squeezie" guide at the top, remove the thread from it first.

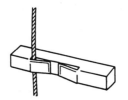

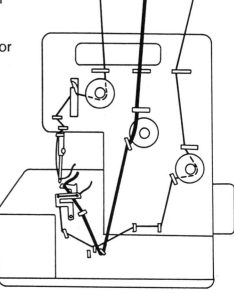

OUR BEST TENSION TIP OF ALL

After teaching several four-day workshops, we discovered the obvious. The WIDTH of the loops is controlled by tension. **Looper** width can be changed by loosening or tightening tension.

In this drawing of a balanced stitch, the loops "hug" the edge of the fabric.

Here, we've loosened the looper tensions. The loops widen and hang over the edge of the fabric.

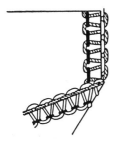
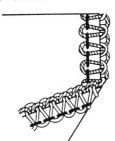

If you actually **change stitch width**, you will move the needle or knife blades. In addition, you will need to change the tensions as follows:

The **wider** the stitch, the **more** looper thread you'll need. Loosen both looper tensions and let more thread flow through.

The **narrower** the stitch, the **less** thread you'll need. Tighten the tension dials to let less thread flow through.

If you **widen** the stitch without loosening the tension, you may get the "pokies" on a woven fabric. The loops are too tight (narrow) against the edge. Loosen the looper tensions.

If you **narrow** the stitch width without tightening the tension, you may get "sloppy" loops or they may hang over the edge too far. Tighten the looper tensions.

When tension is **unbalanced**, a wide loop may even wrap over the edge. Often it is "pulled" over the edge by a narrow loop. Look at the following examples. Which loops need to be narrower? Which ones need to be wider? Always loosen the one that's too tight first!

Loosen (widen) the lower looper tension. You may then need to tighten the upper looper tension.

Loosen the upper looper tension. You may then need to tighten the lower looper tension.

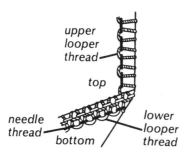

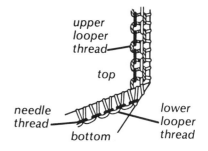

CREATE A REVERSIBLE EDGE

There are times when your heavy decorative thread will **only** work in the upper looper. To make the edge look the same on both sides, loosen the upper looper tension until it "wraps" the edge and tighten the lower looper tension until the lower looper thread disappears. With a 2-thread stitch, tighten the needle and loosen the looper.

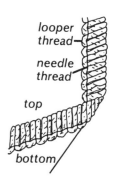

STITCH LENGTH AFFECTS TENSION

If you maintain the same stitch width, but change the length, you will need to change the looper tensions as follows:

The **longer** the stitch, the more looper thread you'll need. **Loosen** the looper tensions so more thread flows through.

The **shorter** the stitch length, the less looper thread you'll need. **Tighten** the looper tensions so less thread flows through.

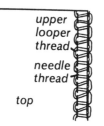

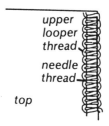

HICCUPS (NARROW STITCHES)

Sue came up with the term "hiccups" for the narrowing of a stitch. This is caused by serging too fast, the thread getting caught in a thread guide, or the thread getting caught on the spool and not reeling off freely.

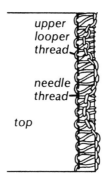

HOW TO FIX HICCUPS

1. Rip out stitching to just above the hiccup. You must begin new stitching without a chained tail. Refer to page 47.

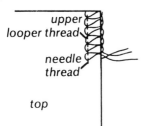

2. Lower needle into seam line a few stitches above where you stopped ripping as shown.

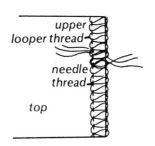

3. When stitching is completed, go back to hiccup area and pull all threads to wrong side. Knot. Dab knots with a seam sealant like Fray Check® or Fray-No-More®. Trim or bury threads in seam.

WHAT HAPPENS IF YOU RUN OUT OF THREAD?

If you are serging along and run out of thread, oh my! However, you can fix the stitching using the same steps for fixing hiccups. You may need to unravel some stitches to have enough to tie, but you won't need to rip out the entire seam.

CREATIVE SERGING *ILLUSTRATED*: NOW YOU TRY!

Remember, we said "Always test first!" Here's your chance to practice what you've learned so far. You will be glad you took the time to put your machine through its paces, so you know what it can and can't do.

For now, work with only two kinds of threads. Later, as you increase the amount of decorative serging you do, you may want to add more test strips to this page.

The four variables you have to work with are:
*type of thread
*stitch width
*stitch length
*needle and looper tensions

1. Cut a piece of study fabric 10" x 30". Draw vertical lines every 1" parallel to the long sides.

2. Choose two threads to test in the upper looper. Use regular sewing thread for the needle(s) and bottom looper.

3. For each thread, run four lines of stitching: (A) wide width; (B) narrow width; (C) short to long stitch length in either width; (D) loose to tight tension in the upper looper. Stop every 5" and look at both sides of the strip, adjusting the tension until you achieve the look you want.

4. (Optional) Make notes in the space below or directly on the sample to help you when you want to use a specific thread on a project. But don't forget: always test first!

		TENSIONS				STITCH	
		NEEDLE(S)		LOOPER(S)			
NOTES:	THREAD	LN	RN	UL	LL	Length	Width

(left four lines rayon, right four lines pearl cotton) Wide width, narrow width, long stitch length, loose tension upper looper

Failsafe
Fundamentals

5 • *Failsafe Fundamentals*

In this chapter we'll show you tips that can make a BIG difference in your serging (and sanity!)

REMOVING THREAD FROM THE STITCH FINGER

Frequently you will need to remove the chained tail threads from the stitch finger in order to pull on, release, or separate the threads. Use this technique for:

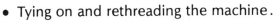

- Separating threads for tying a less bulky knot (see page 50).

- Separating threads to check threading (see page 34).

- Tying on and rethreading the machine.

It's easy! Just pull slack in the **needle thread** between the needle and the tension guide as shown. Pull **slightly** for turning corners and **a lot** for separating threads.

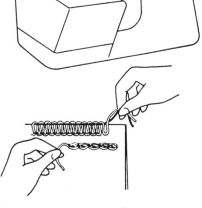

RIPPING STITCHES

- On a 2-thread overedge, pull on needle and looper threads equally and at the same time. They will pull out easily.

- On a 2-thread chain, pull on the looper thread and it will pull right out.

- On 3 and 3/4-thread stitches, slip a small seam ripper under the loops on one side, cutting them. The needle and looper threads on the other side will easily pull out.

KNOTTING NEXT TO THE FABRIC

Pati was a 10-year-old 4-H member when she learned this neat trick for knotting next to the fabric. Our workshop students were awed by this simple method.

1. Tie the knot loosely. Slip a straight pin into its center.

2. Wiggle knot over pin until it gets close to fabric edge.

3. With pin at fabric edge, slip knot to point. Pull tightly.

 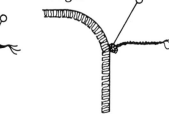

SECURE THE END OF A SEAM BY HAND

The loose loops at the beginning or end of a seam can ravel out. You can't backstitch on a serger! Use one of the following methods to secure a seam:

- **Tie a knot and put a dab of seam sealant** such as Fray Check® or Fray-No-More® on it. After it dries, cut off the excess chain. (Use rubbing alcohol to remove unwanted seam sealant).

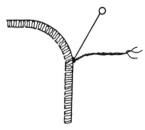

NOTE: To make the seam sealant more "controllable", use a pin or your finger to dab it onto the knot. Sue puts hers into an empty nail polish bottle and uses the brush to apply it.

- **Bury the chain.**

1. Thread it through a large blunt pointed tapestry needle or a loop turner.

2. Pull the chained tail under the looper threads and cut off any excess.

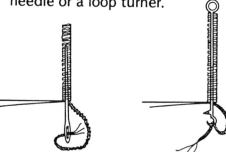 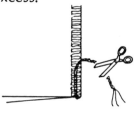

SECURE THE END OF A SEAM BY MACHINE

It's easy and if you follow our instructions carefully, you won't get a loop of chained tail threads on the edge of the fabric as shown at the right.

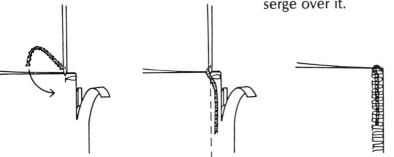

• At the beginning of a seam

1. Stitch one stitch into fabric edge.

2. **Then** lift presser foot and bring chain to front.

3. Pull on chain to make it narrow. Place on seam allowance and serge over it.

• At the end of a seam

1. Serge one stitch off the edge of the fabric. Gently slip the chain off stitch finger (pulling a slight amount of slack above needle will make this easier — see page 47). Raise presser foot. Flip fabric over and to the front of the presser foot.

2. Lower the presser foot and stitch 1"-2" over last few stitches. Be careful not to cut into the stitches already sewn. Chain off and trim the chain.

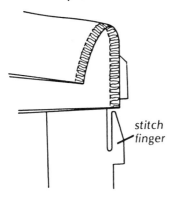

stitch finger

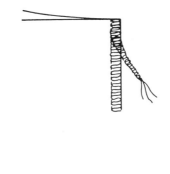

STITCHING IN A CIRCLE

There are two ways to stitch in a circle. However, to entirely avoid serging exposed edges in a circle, use our sewing order, page 58.

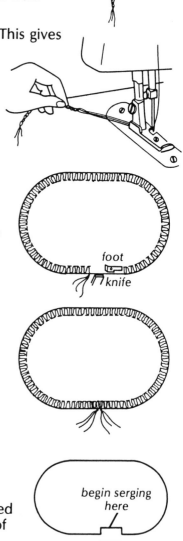

- **Stitch over beginning stitches** 1/2"-1", then off the edge. Tie a knot near the fabric. Put seam sealant on the knot and cut off excess chain. This method can look messy unless you are using a thread that covers well; therefore, we generally reserve it for hem edge finishing.

- **Stitches meet without overlapping.** This gives neater results but takes practice!

1. Pull out unchained threads (see page 47), important if you want a tiny invisible knot.

2. Always begin serging in the **middle** of a long edge, NOT on a curve. **Always** skim the edges with your knives for even width serging. Stop serging when the knives reach the beginning stitches.

3. Raise the upper knife and continue serging **two** stitches over the beginning stitches. This is difficult if you can't raise the knife on your machine.

foot

knife

4. Again, pull out about 3"-4" of unchained tail thread.

5. Tie knots in each tail. Dab knots with seam sealant, then cut off excess thread or weave tails into your serging.

NOTE: Use this technique if you have a seam allowance to trim. Cut away a 2" section of the seam allowance where you plan to begin and end your stitching. Then proceed as above, beginning in the middle of the cutaway.

begin serging here

TURNING INSIDE CORNERS

Inside corners are easier to finish than outside corners. Use the following technique.

1. Serge until the knife touches the corner. Stop with needle in fabric.

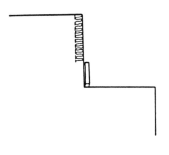

2. Straighten the corner, lifting presserfoot if necessary. You will have a "V" fold of fabric. Don't worry, the pleat will disappear after serging.

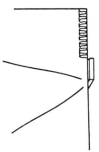

3. Finish serging the straightened edge.

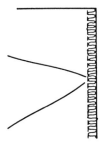

4. Now the inside corner is finished. It will appear a bit rounded.

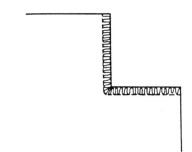

NOTE: If your inside corner has a seam allowance that needs to be trimmed away, simply mark the cutting line within 1" of both sides of the corner using a washable marker. Clip to corner. Serge, as above, trimming off seam allowance.

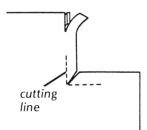

cutting line

TURNING OUTSIDE CORNERS

Pati's mother-in-law learned to sew on a serger by making flannel receiving blankets. She got lots of practice turning corners! Try the following technique:

1. Serge up to the corner and off the edge ONE stitch.

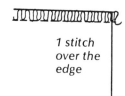

1 stitch over the edge

2. Raise the needle out of the fabric.

3. Pull a small amount of slack in the needle thread — a little finger's worth! This will help you remove the fabric from the stitch finger. Be careful. Too much slack will leave a loop on the corner. Experiment until you determine the right amount of slack required. If you accidentally pull too much, pull the thread back just above the tension dial.

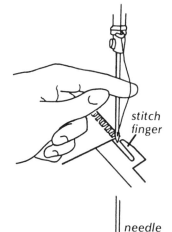

stitch finger

4. Pivot the fabric. Lower the needle into the fabric **BEFORE** lowering the presser foot, or the needle won't end up where you want it! The needle should be in from the edge the same distance as the width of the seam allowance. Place it between the top edge and the seamline of the first stitching.

needle position

5. Continue sewing next edge.

NOTE: If there is a seam allowance, trim it away for 2″ before serging to corner. Remember, your knife is in front of the needle, so you can't turn a corner without first removing the seam allowance!

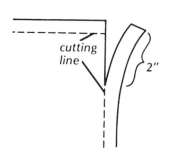

cutting line

2″

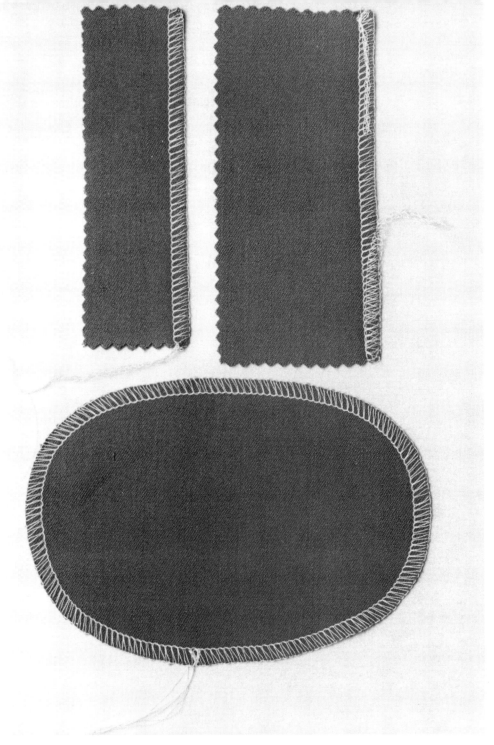

(top left) Chain is knotted next to fabric; (top right) beginning and end of seam are secured by machine; (bottom) each unchained tail thread has been separately knotted and is ready for weaving into serging or being secured with seam sealant.

CREATIVE SERGING *ILLUSTRATED*: HOW GOOD IS GOOD?

Beginners often worry too much about starting and ending serger threads, as if these parts of a garment were projected on a wide-screen TV. Relax: no one but your mother will notice how well you secure threads. The eyes of your adoring public will be on the overall effect of your color, style, personality. (Besides, have you ever looked at the joins on ready-to-wear? Sloppy, yet you wear these clothes without a thought.)

But you can minimize a clumsy look by practicing on small samples the five major ways to start and finish threads. Try each method at least twice, with two different weights of thread in the upper looper—regular sewing thread and pearl cotton. By working in both weights, you'll be able to see why you might choose one method over another—for example, tying a knot in pearl cotton is too bulky.

1. Tie an overhand knot next to the fabric.

2. Dab seam sealant on the edge. After it dries, cut off the excess chain.

3. Bury the chain.

4. Secure the beginning and end by machine. (See page 49.)

5. Tie knots in each tail. Then secure with seam sealant and cut off or weave into the serging threads.

Pin your samples to this page. On the next page you can study close-ups of endings. And on the last page of the book, we've repeated instructions on how to start and end thread, in case you wish to post the information by your machine. Never again should you worry!

6 • *Stabilizing Decorative Serging*

Serging is more durable and the stitch width more consistent, when the edge or seam is stabilized. Without stabilizing, some exposed seams and edges, particularly on knits, can stretch out and ripple when serged, worn or laundered. Gail noticed this on several of her daughter's single-layer tee-shirts; the serged necklines soon stretched or popped out. Our Serger Workshop students have also realized better results with stabilizing — more uniform stitches and less stretching.

Stabilizing isn't always necessary. If in doubt, test on scraps of your project fabric cut on the same grain.

STABILIZING DECORATIVE (EXPOSED) SEAMS

Before deciding whether a seam or edge needs stabilizing, consider the serging stitch. Most stable is the 4/2-thread stitch (chainstitch plus overedge), and the stretchiest are the 3/4- and 3-thread overlock. Generally, the wider the stitch, the more stable the seam.

NOTE: A close satin stitch can cause stretching of a seam or edge, due to thread density.

To stabilize shoulder, neckline, front **seams** or seams in any problem area, try one of the following:

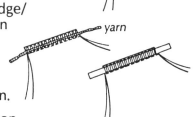

- Sew seam with a row of conventional straight stitching first, then serge seam allowances together. Or, add the straight row after serging.

- Serge using a 4/2-thread overedge/chainstitch. (We have even seen **exposed** 4/2-thread seams on ready-to-wear denim!)

- Serge over braid, ribbon, yarn, buttonhole twist or pearl cotton.

- Flatlock over 1/8" braid or ribbon.

NOTE: For additional stability, press serged seams to one side and edgestitch to garment to secure.

STABILIZING DECORATIVE (EXPOSED) EDGES

There are several ways to stabilize stretch-prone edges.

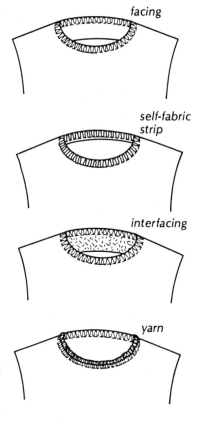

facing

self-fabric
strip

interfacing

yarn

- **Facings** — Cut facings from self- or contrast fabric. Wrong sides together, serge to garment. After serging, leave the facing full width or trim to 1/2"-1". Interface facing with a lightweight fusible for extra body.

- **Narrow self-fabric strips** — Serge 3/4"-1" strips of self-fabric to garment edges wrong sides together. Trim excess to serging. Use lengthwise grain for stability and bias when give is desired.

- **Fusible knit** — 3/4"-1" wide strips of Stacy's Easy Knit or similar fusible tricots are great for adding **both** body **and** stability to an edge or to back an entire piece.

- **Yarn, pearl cotton, buttonhole twist, elastic cord** — Serge over any of these. Tails can be drawn up, easing to fit. Secure tails with a knot and weave under loops on wrong side (see page 48). This technique stabilizes, but doesn't add body. We prefer it when the silhouette demands softness like an angora sweater, or the fabric is stable like boiled wool. A special foot such as a tape sewing or cording foot makes this easier. Otherwise practice feeding the cord through the hole of your regular foot, laying it just to the left of the knife. This is easier than placing it under the foot.

- **Ribbons** — Use ribbons only on straight or slightly curved edges. Place ribbon on wrong side of fabric and serge with ribbon on top. Avoid cutting the ribbon. Serge **over** narrow 1/8"-1/4" ribbon and **through** wider ones.

narrow   **wide**

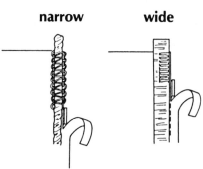

Fast Flat
Construction

CHAPTER 7 · *Fast Flat Construction*

Flat construction is perfect for single layer and reversible clothes. It eliminates serging in a circle. Start with casual tops, then serge ahead to jackets and coats!

SLEEVELESS ROUND NECK PULLOVER TOPS AND DRESSES

Use single layer (or double for reversible looks) of interlock, double-knit, single-knit, or lightweight woven fabric and the following sewing order.

Be sure to stabilize exposed edges if necessary. Serge fabric right or wrong side together as follows:

1. Serge one shoulder seam.

2. Serge to finish the neckline.

3. Serge the other shoulder seam. Then finish armhole edges.

4. Serge one underarm seam and then serge finish hem edge.

5. Serge the other underarm seam. Tie and bury any chain tail threads (see page 48). If desired, topstitch exposed **seams** flat.

"V"-NECKLINE PULLOVER TOPS

Add a center front seam to make
continuous decorative serging easy
on "V"-neck tops. Serge fabric right
or wrong sides together as follows:

1. Serge both shoulder seams.

2. Serge finish the neckline.

3. Serge the center front seam
right or wrong sides
together, whichever you
prefer. If you serge neckline
and front in direction of
arrows, serging can be
continuous.

4. Serge armhole seams. Then
stitch one underarm seam
and serge finish the hem
edge.

5. Now serge the other underarm seam. Tie and bury any chain tail
   threads (see page 48). If desired, topstitch exposed seams
   flat.

SINGLE LAYER JACKETS AND COATS

Who would have ever thought a jacket or coat could be as simple to sew as a blouse? Look for stable meltons, double-knit, double-faced or boiled wool, sweaterknit, or even upholstery fabric. Two medium-weight fabrics in contrasting colors can be used wrong sides together to simulate the look of double-faced fabrics. Use a balanced stitch and the same thread in both loopers or wrap the edge (see page 42). This will make the edge reversible.

GAIL'S FIVE-STEP JACKET (OR COAT)

Gail made this jacket from a very heavy wool melton which is inherently ravel-resistant, making the single layer garment very durable and easy to sew.

1. Decoratively serge finish the outer edges of the upper collar. Serge the shoulders and one underarm seam right sides together.

2. Starting at the lower edge of the open side seam, decoratively serge hem, front edge, collar to neckline, other front and rest of hem.

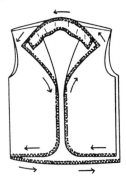

3. Sew the open side seam.

4. Decoratively serge finish the sleeve hem. Seam and set in sleeves.

5. Sew buttons and buttonholes. VOILA! . . . a finished jacket!

MARTA'S LAPPED VARIATION

Palmer/Pletsch's resident sewing speed demon, Marta Alto, has devised another single layer sewing order for coats and jackets.

1. Decoratively serge finish all edges of collar.

2. Serge shoulders and one underarm seam wrong sides together.

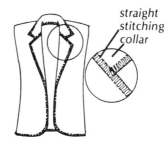

3. Starting at open side seam, decoratively serge finish jacket edges as shown. Serge other side seam wrong sides together.

4. Lap collar and neckline edges, aligning the serged needle lines. Topstitch collar to neckline with a conventional machine.

straight stitching collar

COORDINATE OTHER DESIGN DETAILS

We generally reserve dramatic **contrasting** decorative stitching for lapels, collars, and hemlines. However, when the color matches or is a subtle contrast, other design details can also be decoratively serged, like the edges of:

- Belts
- Patch pockets
- Sleeves
- Back vents
- Yokes

NOTE: Coordinate buttons too! See page 114 for the "wrapped" button.

HALF SLIP OR STRAIGHT KNIT SKIRT

1. Serge one side seam.

2. Serge elastic to the waistline.

3. Serge lace to slip hem, or serge to finish skirt hem.

4. Serge the other side seam. If applies, hem skirt.

5. For skirt only: Fold over top of skirt, encasing elastic, and top-stitch casing.

PULL-ON PANTS OR SWEAT PANTS (WITH OR WITHOUT SIDE SEAMS)

1. If applies, serge side seam.
2. Serge ribbing to, or serge-finish pants hem edge.

3. Serge inseams.

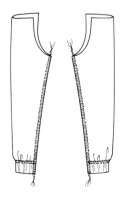

4. Serge the crotch seam.

5. Serge elastic to the top edge (waistline).

6. Fold over top of pants, encasing elastic, and topstitch casing.

RAGLAN SLEEVE PULLOVER OR SWEATSHIRT

1. Serge all but one back sleeve seam.
2. Then serge ribbing to neckline and sleeves.

3. Serge the back sleeve seam through neckline rib.

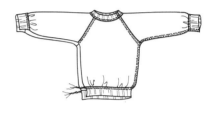

4. Serge one underarm seam.

5. Serge the ribbing to the hem.
6. Serge other underarm seam.

SET-IN SLEEVE PULLOVER OR SWEATSHIRT

1. Sew one shoulder seam. Apply neckline ribbing.

2. Serge other shoulder seam. Set in sleeves. Apply sleeve ribbing.

3. Serge one underarm seam. Apply lower ribbing, or hem.
4. Serge other underarm seam.

Fun With Flatlocking

To brighten the color contrast and increase thread density, Sue Green serged the flatlocked topstitching (see page 69) and seams, using red topstitching thread in the upper looper (see Chapter 8).

(Left) A two-thread rolled edge adds color to this charming child's dress. All edges of the mother's dress are also finished with a black rolled edge.

(Above) All seaming on this shirt was done wrong sides together, with the narrow rolled-edge serging exposed. Edge finishing matches, making even shorter work of Palmer/Pletsch's three-hour shirt (see Chapter 9).

The seam that joins the woven and knit cottons on this top is highlighted with decorative flatlocking. Worked over a conventional sewing-machine seam, pink pearl cotton was used in the upper looper. See Chapter 8.

8 · Fun With Flatlocking

Flatlocking is serging two layers of fabric together, then pulling them apart until the seam lies flat. Since writing our first book **Sewing With Sergers**, we have experimented with flatlocking even more and have been amazed by the possibilities!

We'll show you how to flatlock with either a 2- or 3-thread stitch. A 2-thread flatlock will lie flatter, but a 3-thread stitch adds durability.

Woven fabrics can be flatlocked, but they won't be as durable as knits unless stabilized (see page 67). For your first flatlocking project, try sweatshirting or polar fleece. These fabrics are easy to sew, inexpensive, and durable.

FLATLOCKING IS REVERSIBLE

Depending on whether the fabric is serged right or wrong sides together, there will be **loops or a ladder** (trellis) on the right side.

For **loops** on the right side, flatlock fabric **wrong** sides together. Then pull until the seam lies flat.

For a **ladder** on the right side, flatlock fabric **right** sides together. Then pull until the seam lies flat.

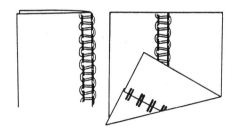

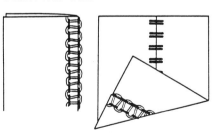

2-THREAD FLATLOCKING

If your machine can sew a
2-thread stitch as shown at the right,
you can sew a 2-thread flatlock.
Check your manual. Opened flat it
will look like the drawings on the
bottom of page 65.

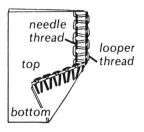

We recommend a balanced tension for a 2-thread flatlock. The
needle and the looper threads should meet at the edge of the fabric.
If using a heavier decorative thread in the looper, the tension may
need to be loosened. Also, if you are flatlocking thick fabrics, both
tensions may need to be loosened. Sew a test sample. If the flatlocking doesn't lie flat, loosen the needle and looper thread tensions
until both hang over the edge slightly.

3-THREAD FLATLOCKING

The following steps allow you to flatlock with a 3-thread stitch:

1. Loosen the needle
tension nearly all the
way and tighten the
lower looper tension.

2. Do this until the needle thread
forms a "V" on the under side and
the lower looper forms nearly a
straight line on the edge.

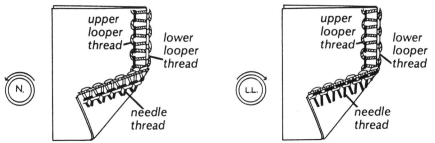

NOTE: If you have tightened the lower looper tension all the
way and still can't get the lower looper thread tight enough,
wrap the thread around the tension dial twice. Loosen the tension, then **gradually** tighten while serging **slowly** so you won't
bend the lower looper. The Bernette serger has an **extra** tension dial for rolled hems, which can also be used for
flatlocking.

Flatlocking will always appear flat-
test when the loops and the ladder
are the same width. If one side
buckles under the stitches, loosen
that tension dial. Do not **overpress** to
try to flatten the stitches!

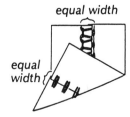

CREATIVE THREAD IDEAS FOR FLATLOCKING

Frame the stitch — When the loops are on the right side, use a contrasting color thread in the needle of a 2-thread stitch or the needle and lower looper of a 3-thread stitch. Your loops will be "framed".

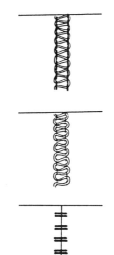

Float the stitch — When the loops are on the right side, use clear filament nylon or matching lightweight thread in the needle of a 2-thread stitch or the needle and lower looper of a 3-thread stitch. The loops will seem to be "floating" on top of the fabric.

Define the ladder — When the ladder or trellis is on the right side, it will always be soft because only lighter weight threads can be used in the needle. Try topstitching thread for a more defined ladder.

FLATLOCKING FABRICS THAT RAVEL

It is easiest and neatest to flatlock on knits because they don't ravel. Even stable wovens may eventually ravel after many wearings and washings. Use one of the following methods to stabilize them:

Method I

1. Sew flatlock seam.

2. **Gently** pull seam flat and press.

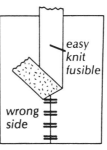

3. Fuse 1" strips of Easy Knit fusible tricot interfacing to the wrong side, centered over the stitches.

4. If more strength is needed, top-stitch from the right side through all layers on both edges of your serging. This will prevent ravelling during repeated washings.

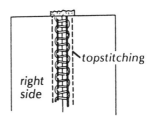

Method II

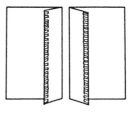

1. Fold seam allowances to wrong side and press. Serge edges of seam allowances.

2. Serge the fabric right or wrong sides together, depending on whether you want the loops or the ladder on the right side of the garment.

3. Pull the layers until the seam is flat. Lightly press.

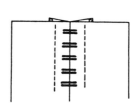

4. As an added decorative touch and for more durability, topstitch the seam allowances flat on both sides of the serging.

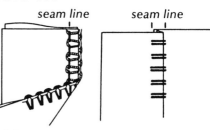

HOW FLATLOCKING AFFECTS FIT

If you flatlock with the needle in the seamline, then pull the seam flat, the garment width will be increased by the width of the seam allowance or about 1/4"-3/8" per seam.

If exact fit is crucial, take a wider seam, increasing it by half the stitch width or about 1/8"-3/16".

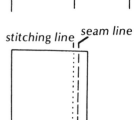

FLATLOCKING FOR A TOPSTITCHED LOOK

Flatlock anywhere on a garment including on a fold. You can even flatlock across flatlocking! Use decorative thread for more stitch definition. This is a great way to dress up sweatshirts or tops **and** to practice your flatlocking.

Fold the fabric and flatlock, being careful not to cut the fold with the serger knives. If possible, raise or remove the knives. However, we use the knives as a stitching guide and seldom remove them. They force us to sew straight!

Loops out

Ladders out

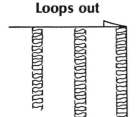

FLATLOCK OVER RIBBON

~ribbon

Flatlock on the fold over ribbon. 1/16"-1/8" width works well because the ribbon should be slightly narrower than the stitch.

This is a great look on blouses and also a pretty embellishment for children's clothes.

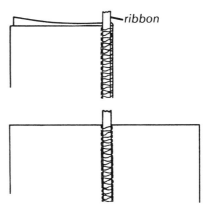

Apply rows to a bodice or just above a ruffle.

FLATLOCK GATHERING

Narrow, center-gathered ruffles are a nice accent above a flounce on a full skirt or curtains. The ruffle edges can be beautifully hemmed before gathering using a narrow rolled serged hem.

1. Fold fabric in half, right sides together. Serge over cording, being careful not to cut the fold.

2. Pull up the cord and open ruffle. Stitch to fabric on both sides of cord or zigzag down the middle with a conventional machine.

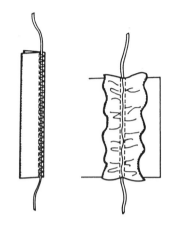

FLATLOCK SHIRRING

Fold the fabric and flatlock over elastic cord.

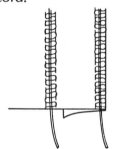

Pull up on the elastic. Flatlock shirr your fabric first.

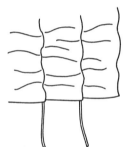

Then cut out your pattern. This is great for children's clothes.

ROLLED EDGE FLATLOCK

Change to a narrow rolled edge stitch. Adjust machine for 2- or 3-thread flatlocking. Flatlock on the fold. The result will look like soutache topstitched onto your fabric. "Frame" the stitch by using contrasting color thread as described on page 67.

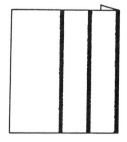

FLATLOCK FRINGE

This is a wonderful finish for scarves, shawls, skirt hems, placemats, and napkins. It looks great when serged with decorative threads. The Coats & Clark educational staff showed us square wool challis print shawls they had flatlocked with black pearl cotton . . . gorgeous and much more finished looking than plain fringing.

Choosing the right fabric is a must. How does the fabric look fringed? Is it loosely woven enough to be easily fringed? If not, choose a more suitable fabric. TEST fringe a scrap first.

To flatlock fringe, do the following:

1. Draw a thread to find the straight of grain on the fabric where your fringe will begin, about 1"-3" from edge.

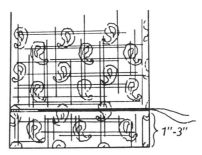

2. Fold your fabric on the drawn thread line.

3. Adjust your serger for flatlocking. Test length and width. Flatlock along the fold of the fabric being careful not to cut the fold (see page 69). As you serge, let the stitches hang halfway over the edge to allow the fabric to pull flat without a tuck forming underneath the stitching.

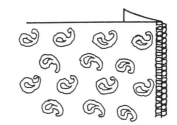

4. Flatten the stitches by pulling on them. Then, fringe to the stitching by gently pulling out all threads lying parallel to the flatlocking.

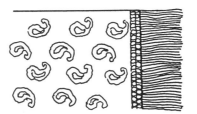

TURNING CORNERS WHEN FLATLOCKING ON THE FOLD

Whether flatlocking or flatlock fringing, use the following steps for turning corners:

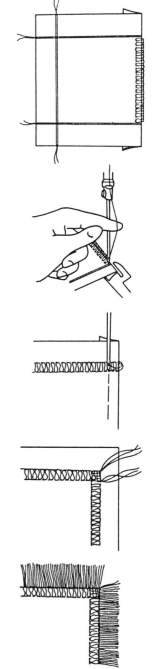

1. Draw threads on all edges to be fringed as described on page 71. Fold the fabric under on drawn thread line and flatlock on fold, beginning where drawn thread lines intersect. Remember, do **not** cut the fold or your fringe will fall off!

2. When you reach the next drawn thread, raise the presser foot, pull slack in the needle thread (see page 47), raise the needle and gently slip the stitches off the stitch finger.

3. Carefully open the first stitching and pull flat. Fold next edge under on drawn thread line. Lower needle in top of first stitching line as shown. **Then**, lower presser foot and flatlock to next drawn thread. Repeat these steps until all edges are finished.

4. On the last edge, stop serging immediately after overlapping the other stitches. Raise the presser foot and the needle. Pull enough slack in the needle to remove the stitches from the stitch finger and pull fabric from machine. Allow enough thread tail length for tying and burying under the stitches.

5. Pull edges flat and fringe to stitching as on page 71.

FLATLOCK DESIGN IDEAS

As a design variation, serge more rows of flatlock topstitching (see page 69) parallel to the flatlocked fringe. Also, vary the look and save time by flatlocking and fringing only one or two sides of a project. For instance, on an oblong scarf, flatlock fringe the short ends first, then finish the longer sides with rolled edges. A skirt hem requires only one row of flatlocked fringing — plus no corners.

FLATLOCK FAGOTING

True fagoting is accomplished by pulling horizontal threads out of a fabric and tying the remaining vertical threads together in hour-glass bunches as shown.

You can achieve a similar look with the serger. For a delicate hand-crafted look, use this technique to join layers of lightweight cotton or handkerchief linen.

1. Serge to finish seam allowances and press to wrong side. Right sides together, flatlock with loops hanging halfway over the edge of fabric.

2. When you pull the seam flat, there will be an even width space between the layers.

3. Weave a shiny 1/8" satin ribbon in and out of the fagoting as a variation.

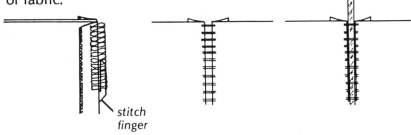

stitch finger

CREATIVE SERGING *ILLUSTRATED:*
FLATLOCK SAMPLER

Before you can incorporate all the exciting variations we've presented in this chapter, you must practice making the basic flatlock stitch on *your* machine. Here's a simple sampler quick to make that will give you experience in two of the three variations on page 67.

1. Cut a piece of sturdy fabric 7" x 10" (striped fabric makes it easy to follow lines). You will also need a long scrap for experimentation. (Once you have the tensions set, you will not need to readjust them for the different lines of flatlocking on the permanent record.) Divide the fabric into five vertical equidistant lines. You will also need two colors of buttonhole twist in the needle and loopers.

2. Variation 1: frame the stitch. Load a contrasting thread color in the needle of a 2-thread machine or the needle and lower looper of a 3-thread machine. To test tensions, fold the scrap fabric and serge, following the tension settings suggested on page 66. Adjust tensions until you achieve the look you want. Write settings below. Then work the far left and right lines on your permanent record, folding the fabric wrong sides together. You do not need to trim the fold.

3. Variation 2: define the ladder. Turn the fabric over and work the second and fourth lines from the left. When you pull the fabric flat, the ladder will be visible on the topside. (Buttonhole twist gives a more pronounced ladder than regular sewing thread.)

4. Change all threads to the same color and work the last two lines of flatlocking from the topside. If you were to use clear nylon in the needle and lower looper, you would achieve variation 3, floating the stitch.

NOTES:	THREAD	TENSIONS					
		NEEDLE(S)		LOOPER(S)		STITCH	
		LN	RN	UL	LL	Length	Width

(l to r, first three lines) The needle thread on a 2-thread serger frames the stitch; buttonhole twist gives a more pronounced ladder than regular sewing thread; all threads are the same color.

The Perfect Rolled Edge

CHAPTER 9 · The Perfect Rolled Edge

One of our favorite features on a serger is the rolled edge. Garments like blouses are now easy to sew and professional looking. Save money on children's clothes and use self-fabric ruffles instead of lace. Gail, the home decorating expert, now uses the rolled edge to neatly and quickly finish curtain tiebacks, tablecloths and napkins, and ruffled pillows. It is also very durable because the fabric actually rolls under.

Our first book describes rolled edge basics. Now we want to elaborate on the how-tos, the decorative uses of the rolled edge stitch, and the problems you may encounter when venturing on to more challenging fabrics and threads.

SETTING UP YOUR MACHINE

You will need a narrow stitch finger to sew a rolled edge. On some machines this adjustment is built-in; on others you need to change throat plates. You may also need to change to a special presser foot. Check your manual.

The edge of the fabric actually rolls under because the distance between the knives and the stitch finger is greater than the width of the stitch by at least 1/8".

Set your stitch width to 2mm or narrower if possible. We recommend **gradually** shortening the stitch length until you get the look desired. Most people prefer a satin stitch, but beginning on a very short length may cause uneven feeding of fabric and a lumpy edge. TEST on a sample first!

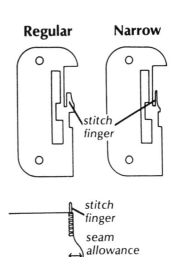

Regular   **Narrow**

stitch finger

stitch finger

seam allowance

knife

Fabric is always placed on your machine right side up except when serging a fabric that rolls to the right side like crosswise grain tricot. Why fight it? Place it right side down.

NARROW EDGE VS. NARROW ROLLED EDGE

In machine manuals, you see the terms narrow edge and narrow rolled edge. There is a difference. In both cases the fabric rolls because of the distance between the knife and the narrow stitch finger. However, the narrow edge does roll a bit less. The difference is caused by tension adjustments.

On a **narrow edge** the stitch is balanced. The upper and lower looper threads of a 3-thread stitch and the needle and looper threads of a 2-thread stitch meet at the edge.

For a **narrow rolled edge**, the stitch is unbalanced. The upper looper thread of a 3-thread stitch and looper thread of a 2-thread stitch encases the edge.

TENSION ADJUSTMENTS FOR A 3-THREAD ROLLED EDGE

Lower looper — The greatest tension adjustment is on the lower looper. By tightening it nearly all the way, the lower looper thread will become a straight line on the wrong side of the fabric and nearly disappear. It also pulls the upper looper thread to the underside.

Tighten lower looper a lot.

NOTE: If you can't get the lower looper thread tight enough, you aren't alone. This is a common problem. In our workshops, our students have solved this by wrapping the tension dial twice. Do this at your own risk, however, as it is not recommended in the manuals. After wrapping, loosen the tension and begin sewing slowly to make sure you don't overstress the looper and cause it to break. Gradually tighten the dial again if necessary.

Upper looper — It may need a little tightening or loosening, but depends on the type of thread and fabric used as well as stitch length. Since decorative threads are generally used **only** in the upper looper, TEST on a sample first.

No change but test.

Needle — The needle thread tends to loosen under the strain, so you may need to tighten the tension. If it becomes **too** tight, however, the edge may pucker. TEST on a sample first. Puckering most often occurs on the lengthwise grain of fabric.

Tighten needle a little.

The following drawings show you how a rolled edge is formed:

As you tighten the lower looper tension, the upper looper is brought to the wrong side.	As the lower looper becomes tighter, it creates stress on the needle thread. Tighten it.	Perfect! The upper looper has been pulled all the way to the under side and the needle thread is hidden.

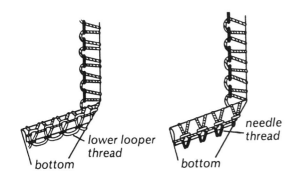
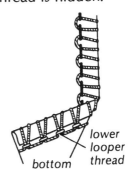

TENSION ADJUSTMENTS FOR A 2-THREAD ROLLED EDGE

If your serger sews a 2-thread stitch and can make a rolled edge, try it for a lighter edge finish. Bridal veils are often finished this way. Adjust your machine for a rolled edge per your instruction manual.

Tighten the needle tension until the looper thread rolls from the top of the fabric to the underside and encases the edge. If the fabric is heavy, you may need to tighten the upper looper also to make the fabric roll.

Tighten needle tension.

**Narrow edge—
Balanced 2-thread tension**

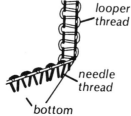

**Narrow rolled edge—
unbalanced 2-thread tension**

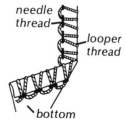

DECORATIVE ROLLED EDGES

variegated threads

Make a rolled edge more decorative by using a contrasting or special thread. Rayon, silk, and metallics add shine. Woolly Nylon adds texture and gives good coverage. Variegated threads are beautiful because they "color block". Generally, finer threads (extra fine, serger, or regular thread) are better. However, you can try topstitching thread for more definition. Pearl cotton, crochet threads, and yarn will generally be too bulky. TEST them using a longer stitch length.

ROLLED EDGE STITCH VARIATIONS

Picot, Shell, or Scalloped Edge

This look, commonly seen in lingerie, is formed by lengthening the stitch to 5, 6, or 7mm. If the fabric puckers, loosen the needle tension. The fabric can be held taut both in front of and behind the presser foot to prevent puckering.

Mini Blanket Stitch Look

Loosen the needle and tighten both loopers nearly all the way. Both looper threads will be on the edge of the fabric and the needle thread will show on both sides. Lengthen the stitch to 5mm. The result will look like a narrow blanket stitch. Try this with lightweight decorative threads in the needle and loopers.

Lettuce Leaf Edging

This ruffled or "lettuce" effect can be interesting on belts, aerobic wear and skirts. Create a lettuce effect with any narrow or rolled edge set on a short satin stitch length. The degree of ruffling is based on the amount the edge will stretch. The following will affect stretch:

- Use stretchier fabrics such as single knits and jerseys.

- Lightweight fabrics will lettuce more than heavy weight.

- Crosswise grain in knits and bias in wovens will stretch more.

- The shorter the stitch length, the more lettuce effect you'll get.

- Increase presser foot pressure to increase stretching.

CREATIVE USES FOR THE ROLLED EDGE STITCH

Rolled Edge Scallops

This technique is great for fabrics or lace.

1. Trim away seam allowances on scallops.

2. Disengage knife. If you can't, don't try this technique. Serge edge of scallops with rolled edge stitch. When you reach the inside point between scallops, straighten the fabric as you would for an inside corner (see page 51). Do not stretch.

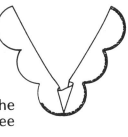

Attaching Laces and Trims

Use the rolled hem stitch to attach laces and trims for a corded edge appearance. Place lace and fabric wrong sides together and serge together with the rolled hem stitch.

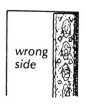

wrong side

Decorative Belt Loops or Lattice Work

Create decorative strips of fabric for belt loops or lattice work. They can also be woven together for pillows, handbags, yokes and other accents.

lattice

belt loops

1. Cut long strips of fabric 1″ wide. Later the strips can be cut into the lengths needed. Interface to prevent stretch if necessary. Fuse the strips wrong sides together with fusible web for extra body and for easier handling.

2. Serge along one edge with a rolled edge stitch. Turn the strip around, making sure the same side is on top. Align the first stitching with the left side of your presser foot for even width strips. Serge the other side.

3. Cut the strip into lengths desired.

Make Your Own Trim

When you can't find trim to match your fabric, make your own. Use lace, eyelets, cotton blends — the sky's the limit!

1. Cut strips of fabric the width desired plus a seam allowance. If gathering the trim cut it three times the finished length.

2. Serge one edge with a rolled edge stitch. Attach to garment flat or after gathering.

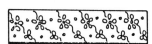

Create Your Own Piping

By making your own piping with the rolled edge stitch, you will be able to match almost any color of fabric. You can create an unusual lightweight look not available in purchased piping.

1. Cut bias strips of chiffon 2" wide. The bias adds flexibility to the finished piping.

2. Place one to three strands of filler cord such as pearl cotton in the center of the bias strip. Fold bias strip in half over filler cords.

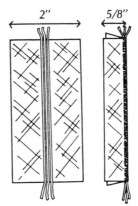

3. Serge over the filler threads with a rolled edge stitch. Trim seam allowance to 5/8".

VOILA! Piping! Insert while sewing a seam or facing an edge. Using a zipper foot, stitch close to piping. See our **Sensational Silk** book for complete piping instructions.

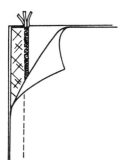

CREATIVE USES OF THE CHAIN TAIL THREAD

The rolled edge chain itself looks very nice, especially when using a heavier thread like topstitching thread. Every time you use the rolled edge stitch, serge an extra yard for belt carriers, button loops, or spaghetti straps.

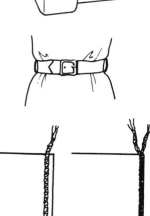

Belt Loops

Pull on the chain to smooth out the loops. See our book **Sewing With Sergers** for tips on attaching chain belt loops.

Filler Cord

If you want your rolled hem stitch to be fuller and stiffer, use a matching length of chain as a filler cord. Smooth out excess loops in the chain by pulling it taut. Place the chain on top of the fabric and serge over it with a rolled edge stitch.

DECORATIVE ROLLED EDGE SEAMS

Seams Out

Try seaming lightweight fabrics wrong sides together using a rolled edge stitch. Decorative matching or contrasting threads are lovely.

Serge with the two layers of fabric wrong sides together. To prevent raveling, a short stitch length (satin stitch) is best.

Seams in Sheers and Laces

Rolled edge seams look gorgeous showing through sheers and laces. These are considered decorative because they show. Gail likes to use Woolly Nylon for softness and better thread coverage.

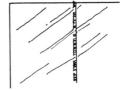

To stabilize loosely woven or stretch fabrics, place a 1/2" wide strip of sheer tricot like Seams Great® or Seams Saver® on top of the seam and stitch through all three layers. Trim the excess tricot close to the seamline when finished.

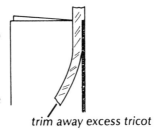

trim away excess tricot

SOLUTIONS TO ROLLED EDGE PROBLEMS

Students in our workshops seem to have some problems over and over. Because they are common, we'd like to address them here.

Stitches Do Not Cover the Edge

This is most common when the thread and fabric are different colors. Shorten the stitch length; try two strands of regular thread in the upper looper; or use Woolly Nylon as it fluffs and spreads to fill in the spaces between the stitches.

Stitches Pull Away From the Edge of the Fabric

If the fabric is loosely woven, the rolled edge may pull off the fabric. This happens most often on the crosswise grain of the fabric. Lengthening the stitch will help as fewer needle holes will be punched into the fabric. Also, use the smallest needle available for your serger.

Another option is to move the knife farther away from the stitch finger so that more fabric is being rolled into the edge. This can be done on most machines; however, consult your owner's manual.

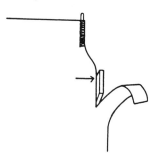

Our last resort is to serge over tricot to stabilize as shown on page 85. Trim tricot to seamline when finished.

The Rolled Edge "Pokeys"

"Pokeys" are little fibers sticking out the edge like whiskers. This most often happens with heavier or stiffer woven fabrics that resist rolling. Try moving the knives to the right so more fabric rolls under. Check your owner's manual to see if this is possible.

"pokeys"

It is almost impossible to control "pokeys" on metallic wovens. Place a strip of sheer tricot such as Seams Saver or Seams Great on **top** of the fabric and serge through all layers. Trim the excess tricot close to stitching with embroidery scissors.

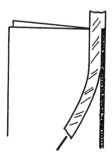

When all other attempts fail, try folding under the raw edge about 3/8" to the wrong side. Align the fold just to the left of the knives. Being careful not to cut the fold, serge along the edge.

trim away excess tricot

Using sharp embroidery scissors, trim away the excess fabric to the stitching.

Reverse "Pokeys"

When you see pokeys on the **inside** of the rolled edge, it means too much was rolled into it for the type of fabric you are working with. If possible, move the knives to the left, so more fabric is trimmed.

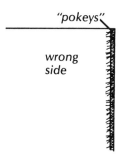

"pokeys"

wrong side

Rolled Edge Puckers

Loosen the needle tension. Then try a smaller needle. Also, if the stitch length is too short, the stitches will stack on top of each other and sometimes cause puckers.

Also, if you do not let the machine trim at least a small amount off the edge, you will have spots with less fabric in the roll and it can cause unevenness and puckers. Therefore, **always** let the knives trim off a small amount.

Fabric Won't Roll

If the fabric is stiff or heavy, it may not roll. It will scrunch instead, resulting in the "pokeys". You can tighten the upper looper, forcing a roll. If that doesn't work, loosen your upper looper and you will eliminate the pokeys, but produce a wider edge finish.

Rolled Edge is Stiff and Heavy

If you want a lighter rolled edge, use a lighter weight thread such as rayon, silk, machine embroidery thread, or extra fine thread. You can also lengthen the stitch to reduce the density of the thread.

Rolled Edge is Not Consistent in Density and Width

A rolled edge sometimes looks different in the lengthwise and crosswise grains. There is not much you can do about this (although we have come up with a solution for napkin edges, see below). Preshrinking fabric to remove sizing sometimes promotes more even rolled edge stitching.

The serger always rolls the edge of the fabric down. If your fabric wants to roll up, it will fight the machine and produce an uneven edge. Don't fight it. Place the fabric on the machine so it will roll down.

Dog-eared Corners

You can turn corners with a rolled edge, but generally we just serge off, then begin on the other edge and cross over our first stitching. To secure threads, use a seam sealant on the corners. After it dries, trim off the tails. The sealant is not water-soluble, so the project will be washable.

To avoid dog-eared corners (see top illustration), use Gail's trick.

As she approaches the corner, Gail angles in the last three or four stitches, about 1/8", as shown in center illustration. Then, on the next edge, she begins stitching in a little (about 1/8"), then angles back out (dotted line, lower illustration). The finished appearance is a perfect right-angled corner.

CREATIVE SERGING *ILLUSTRATED*: ROLLED EDGE SAMPLER

Rolled edges are integral to serger sewing — for napkin and tablecloth edgings, for ruffles, for hems. So that you feel no hesitation about easily switching back and forth between standard serging and rolled edges, we encourage you to stop reading, run to your machine, and practice with a variety of threads.

1. The fabric you choose for practice should be lightweight and firmly woven, like lining fabric. Cut two pieces 12" x 30", one for experimentation and one for a permanent record. Draw vertical lines every 1-1/2" parallel to the long edges.

2. Collect a variety of threads for the upper looper, from regular sewing thread to metallic (see caption for suggestions of which threads to try). Use regular serger thread in the needle and lower looper.

3. Check your manual for the settings suggested for your machine. Set the stitch length on the shortest setting. Do not change this setting, so you can examine how the various threads perform at this setting.

4. Load one thread in the upper looper. Fold the far left line on the experimental fabric. Serge along the fold, barely cutting it off. Check the tensions every 5" until you are satisfied. Write the thread you're using and the settings below. Then serge the permanent record.

5. Continue experimenting with your threads, writing your results in the chart below.

| | | TENSIONS | | | | STITCH | |
| | | NEEDLE(S) | | LOOPER(S) | | | |
NOTES:	THREAD	LN	RN	UL	LL	Length	Width

(l to r) Rolled edge: regular thread, topstitching, rayon, woolly nylon, metallic (all on the same length and width).

Heirloom Sewing

CHAPTER 10 · *Heirloom Sewing*

The art of French Handsewing has been revived and it is all the rage among needle artists. When worked by hand, as it was in the Victorian era, the intricate scheme of lace inserts, pintucks, and entredeaux required hours and hours of painstaking sewing.

In this chapter, we'll show you how quickly and beautifully serging can simulate French Handsewing. We call it "Heirloom Serging". You'll love the results for feminine blouses, frilly childrenswear (christening gowns are gorgeous), and for accents such as yokes, pockets, or hankies.

CHOOSING A PATTERN

Styles with minimal darting and seaming are best. Also, generous design ease will afford larger garment sections for heirloom serging. Decoratively serge the fabric first, **then** layout the pattern and cut out the garment. Remember, fit the pattern before cutting out.

HEIRLOOM FABRICS

Heirloom sewing was traditionally worked on delicate Swiss batiste or organdy. Lightweight wovens such as batiste, organdy, and handkerchief linen are widely available today. Recommended fabric color choices for heirloom projects are white, ecru, or pastels. Trim and fabrics should be color-on-color such as white on white or pale pink on pale pink. However, on white you can occasionally add a hint of pastel ribbon or stitching.

CHOOSING FINE THREADS

Finer threads are best for delicate heirloom serging. Try serger or extra-fine machine embroidery thread. A hint of shine from rayon and silk thread can be very pretty. Serge a TEST sample first to check suitability of thread with fabric, trims, and stitches used. Avoid any thread that breaks easily during testing!

TRIMS, LACES, AND RIBBONS

Many laces, trims, and ribbons will serge beautifully. When choosing a lace, it should be soft, but have body; washable, if used in washable garments; the same weight, or heavier than the fabric; and wider than the serger presser foot to avoid bunching. We also like narrow 1/16"-1/8" ribbons under a flatlocked stitch for an accent. The following are some of our favorite laces and trims:

Entredeaux (on-trah-doe) — a trim with 1/16"-1/8" wide holes similar to hemstitching. For serger sewing choose one with fabric borders. Use it between strips of fabric or other laces or trims.

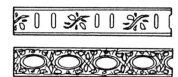

Beading — can be either a lace or embroidered trim. It has openings through which ribbons can be inserted. Try a narrow pastel ribbon for a hint of color.

Lace Insertion — has a straight edge on each side. Packaged lace seam binding is a common example of lace insertion.

Lace Edging — has one straight edge and one scalloped edge. Use the scallop to finish a hem edge.

Untrimmed Eyelet — makes great lace insertion. The untrimmed edges will be straight after serging. Adjust the finished width of the trim as desired.

Fabric Puffing — made from a strip of garment fabric, gathered on **both** long edges and used as an insertion. For a slightly puffed insert, start with a fabric strip twice the finished length. For full puffing, use a strip three times as long.

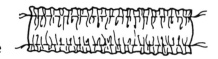

ESTIMATING LACE AND TRIM YARDAGE

To estimate the yardage of each lace and trim you plan to use, determine the length of each row and multiply by the number of rows. Plus, buy extra for practice and mistakes. The pattern envelope may be of some help if it gives back length and hem width measurements.

STITCHES USED IN HEIRLOOM SERGING

- **2- or 3-thread rolled edge stitch** — can be used for:

  inserting laces and trims   **pintucking** (use the width of the presser foot as a guide)

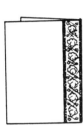 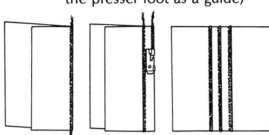

- **Flatlocking** — can be used for:

  joining lace to lace or lace to fabric (loops or ladder can be on right side)   **flatlocking on the fold** (generally done with the ladder on the right side)

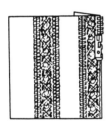

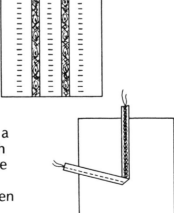

- **Chainstitch** — if your serger will sew a chain, use it to decorate ribbon. With decorative thread in the looper, place the ribbon right side down and sew through the center of the ribbon. Then serge the ribbon to the garment.

- **Regular serged seam** — can be used for sewing tucks (use a wide width satin stitch) or for joining decorative work.

- **Decorative stitches on a conventional machine —**

  To fill in spaces between rows of lace or pintucks, use ribbons, topstitched in place, or rows of embroidery stitches such as flowers, sewn on a conventional machine.

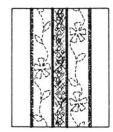

CREATING HEIRLOOM YARDAGE

It is easier to create heirloom yardage first, then cut out your garment. Estimate fabric yardage the same way we suggested estimating yardage of laces and trims. Add an extra 8" of length for blips and glitches.

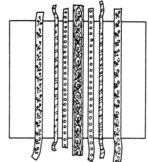

If you are creating yardage just for a collar or a yoke, your strips of fabric and trims should be at least 4" longer than the widest part of the garment piece. This allows for shifting of trims as you serge.

The following tips will save your sanity when creating heirloom yardage:

- All stitching should be done on the lengthwise grain or puckering may occur.

- "Test see" a design by laying strips of the trim, lace, and ribbons over the fabric. Re-arrange until you are satisfied. Note the center, spacing, and order of rows.

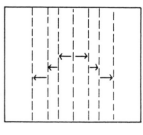

- Lightly mark trim placement lines with a water soluble marker.

- As you build the design, start in the center and add trim to the left, then the right. Do not build all of one side, then try to repeat it on the other side. Both sides would be guaranteed to look different!

- Always sew with lace or trim on top so upper looper thread is in same place on both sides. You will sew from bottom to top on one side and top to bottom on the other.

- If you have a stitching problem and need to rip, remove the entire row of stitching. If the stitching is on the fold like pintucking or flatlocking, be careful not to cut the fabric or you will end up with a hole and the area will be too weak to hold up after restitching.

SEWING ORDER

The following is a sample of a sewing procedure used to create heirloom yardage:

1. Draw center line and insertion lines on fabric with water soluble marker.

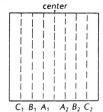

2. Cut on line A_1 and insert trim.

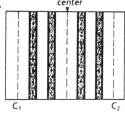

3. Cut on line A_2 and insert trim.

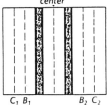

4. Cut on line B_1. Insert trim. Then cut on line B_2. Continue until all trim is inserted.

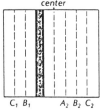

PATTERN LAYOUT

After you have created your heirloom yardage, lay pattern tissue over the design. Shift the pattern over the stitching to determine which placement works best. Cut each garment piece single layer. Don't forget to flip the pattern for a right and left side unless the design is asymmetrical.

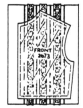
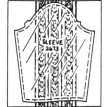

Gail Brown and Naomi Baker designed this simple heirloom serging project, a pincushion about 5" square, finished.

Melissa's dress

96

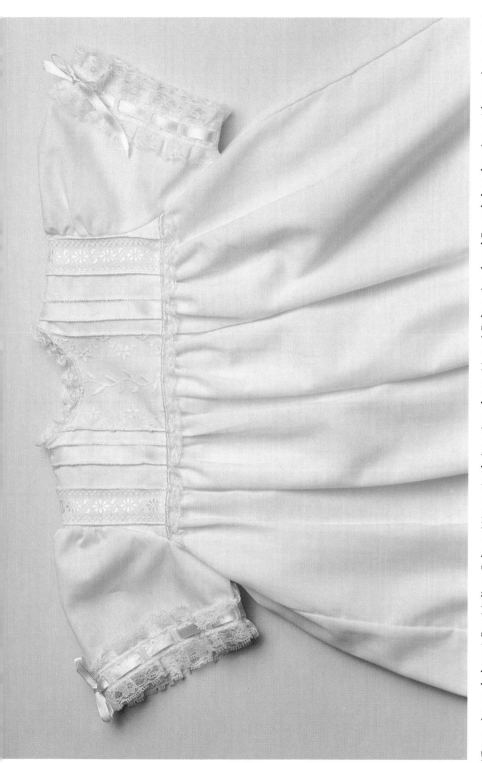

(Opposite and above) For Melissa Palmer-Watson's christening dress, Naomi Baker simulated French handsewing with serging – rayon thread and a narrow rolled edge were used to serge pintucks, lace trim, ribbon and ruffles (see Chapter 10).

Using a serger for seaming, Gail Brown recycled an outdated handknit sweater vest into this jacket. Quilted leather was added for the sleeves, with scraps used for the bottom band and pocket lips.

Virginia Fulcher decided to serge the pink ribbing to the neckline before straight stitching the center front and back seams. For a blouson look, a 9" (finished) hip band hugs the hipline. See Chapter 11.

(Overleaf) Bett Simpson, Gail's daughter, loves doll clothes that match her own, like the matching sweater dresses shown here. Seldom is extra fabric required. See Chapters 11 and 13 for ribbing and sweaterknit how-tos.

Ribbing

CHAPTER **11** · *Ribbing*

Ribbing, the functional finishing for tee's and sweat-shirts, is now seen in the most fashionable places — on wool doubleknit dresses, woven silk blouses, and designer leather jackets. This stretchy knit finishing knows no gender. It's versatile for men's, women's and childrenswear.

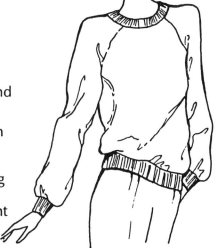

Ribbing is synonomous with serging. Study ready-to-wear ribbing applications. Most are serged. Like the ribbing, serging stretches. Plus, narrow serged seam allowances are lightweight and inconspicuous, perfect for body-fitting ribbed fashions.

With the following tips, anyone can be a ribbing expert. You'll find many creative uses for fast-to-serge ribbing. Have fun!

CHOOSE THE RIGHT RIBBING

When a ribbing application looks homemade, the culprit is generally the ribbing, not the seamstress. Read through this section before shopping and at least you won't **buy** a problem!

- **Avoid sloppy ribbing by TESTING resiliency.** Simply stretch the ribbing firmly. Does it return to its original size? If not, look for another. Words of wisdom from our ribbing expert, Naomi Baker, "Ribbing that stretches out and doesn't stretch back will **always** be ugly no matter how well you sew!"

- **Investigate fiber content.** Care requirements for the ribbing and garment should be the same. Ribbing choices are many — 100% cotton, cotton/Lycra®, cotton/polyester, nylon, acrylic, acrylic/polyester, acrylic/wool, and 100% wool. The ones that are most resilient are cotton/Lycra® (incredible stretch recovery, but hard to find and less ribbed looking), 100% nylon (can be "plastic" feeling), acrylic/wool (the more wool, the more resilient), and 100% wool (gorgeous, versatile, and spendy.)

- **Combine similar weight fabrics and ribbings.** If the ribbing is heavier, it will overpower the fabric. If the ribbing is too lightweight, it won't have the body and resiliency to control the edge. Our favorite ribbing/fabric combinations are wool ribbing on wool doubleknit or silk charmeuse. We also like cotton/polyester ribbing on cotton/polyster interlock knit. Experiment!

- **Know how ribbings are sold.** Most commonly available are 24"-60" wide tubular **ribbings sold by the yard**. 1"-4" wide **ribbed bands** with one finished edge are also available and often coordinated to yardage. Gail's favorite finish for crew neckline tee-shirts is a ribbing band folded wrong sides together and applied double layer for extra body. Rib knit collars are real timesavers, and not for polo shirts only.

Often striped or finished with interesting edgings like picots, rib knit collars are great for perking up a solid color fabric. Buy three collars — one for the neckline and two for the cuffs.

- **Be creative if you can't find MATCHING ribbing.** Consider contrasting colors. Black is elegant on most brights. White is a nice accent on a print. Gail salvages ribbing by trimming it off worn or outdated clothes (some are thrift shop finds). She also knits her own ribbing, especially nice for heavy woolens, leathers or leather-likes.

DO NOT PRESHRINK RIBBING.

Preshrinking ribbing makes it soft and much harder to handle. Only lengthwise shrinkage if any will occur, not significantly affecting the stretch or fit.

RIBBING RATIOS

Ribbing should hug the body and keep the edge of the garment from stretching. Generally all ribbing is stretched at least a little when applied, even to a straight edge. The more curved the edge, the more you will need to stretch the ribbing to make it lie flat and hug the body. Knowing how much to stretch ribbing becomes intuitive for ribbing enthusiasts. Unfortunately for beginners, there are no absolute rules, because there are too many variables.

Ribbing stretched the right amount. Hugs the body.

Ribbing not stretched enough. Stands away from body.

For neckline ribbing that hugs the body, follow these general guidelines:

Round necklines — Cut ribbing 2/3 the size of the neckline and pin in place distributing ease evenly.

Oval necklines — Cut ribbing 3/4 the size of the neckline. Place most of the stretch over the shoulder area. For 5"-7" across center front and back, stretch ribbing only 1/2"-1".

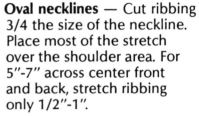

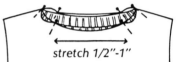

stretch 1/2"-1"

For "V" necklines — Cut ribbing 3/4 the size of the neckline and stretch only slightly down the front.

For turtlenecks — Cut the ribbing the same size as the neckline or slightly less if very tight.

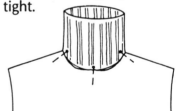

MAKE SURE THE RIBBING WILL FIT

Common sense is a good guide for fitting ribbing. Simply pin the ribbing into a circle and try it on. Does it fit easily over your head, wrist, or waist?

SUE'S TIPS FOR SERGING RIBBING

Sue teaches ribbing application in our serger workshops. Her many helpful hints include:

- **Use either a 3- or 3/4- thread stitch** because they have the most give. Use a medium stitch length and medium to wide width.

- **Lift the presser foot** and put the layers of ribbing and fabric under it. Lower the presser foot and begin sewing.

- **Always serge with the ribbing on top,** with the exception of "V" necklines. See page 103.

- **Follow a flat construction sewing order** to avoid serging in a circle. See pages 102 and 103.

- **When applying ribbing over other serged seams, reinforce those seams** for 1" on a conventional machine. Since a narrow seam allowance is used to apply ribbing, seams can "pop" where they meet ribbing.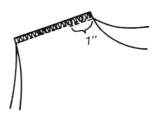

- **Trim all seam allowances on ribbing and garment to 1/4".** This makes it easier to apply ribbing evenly.

- **If you goof, rip out stitches** or in many cases you can serge again, trimming off the first seam. It will make your ribbing narrower, however. You may also serge over first stitching to even up an uneven seam.

- **Press minimally.** Touch the iron to seam allowances only. Pressing can stretch some ribbing. Press over a hem, steaming the ribbing to shape of neckline. Let ribbing cool before moving.

- **Do not use seam sealant** to secure the ends of neckline ribbing seams. When it dries it will be scratchy! Gail discovered this when her daughter, Bett, complained. Knot close to the fabric instead (**see page** 48).

CIRCULAR RIBBING APPLICATION

This is the most common ribbing application, popular in tee shirts and also used on cuffs and waistlines. Our students prefer this tidy technique. The ribbing is seamed in a circle first, then serged on.

1. Cut the ribbing to size.

2. Right sides together, seam the ribbing with a conventional straight stitch. Finger press open.

3. Fold ribbing wrong sides together. To distribute ease evenly, quarter both ribbing and neckline.

4. Match the pins and serge, stretching ribbing to fit garment edge. **Remove** pins as you serge.

5. To end the seam, overlap stitches for about 1″-2″, then taper off the edge.

FLAT CONSTRUCTION IS FASTEST!

1. Serge one shoulder seam.

2. Serge ribbing to neckline edge.

3. Serge other shoulder seam.

4. Serge ribbing to sleeve edges.

5. Serge sleeves to armholes.

6. Serge one underarm seam.

7. Serge ribbing to hem edge.

8. Serge other underarm seam.

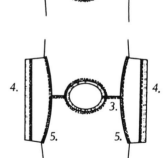

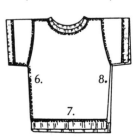

For "V" Necklines

1. Serge one shoulder seam.

2. Serge ribbing to neckline with fabric on top to ensure catching the "V". Use inside corner technique on page 51.

3. Miter the "V" by folding it in half along center front. Machine baste on a conventional machine from serged needle line to ribbing edges. From the right side, make sure the ribbing seams and edges match. Then final stitch with a straight stitch.

4. Clip the miter fold and press back. Hand tack the raw edges flat to the serged seams.

5. Finish garment using crew neckline sewing order.

CREATIVE RIBBING IDEAS

- Lettuce the top edge of double-layer ribbing. Use a narrow rolled edge and Woolly Nylon thread. Stretch as you sew. Lettuce leaf ribbed socks to match!

- For the Esprit look, mix and match ribbing colors on top.

- Pants too short? Serge ribbing to the hem edge. Instant fashion.

- For the "hot hip band" look, cut ribbings super wide, at least 7" when folded in half.

- Apply right side of ribbing to the wrong side of garment neckline. The ribbing will fold over and hide serged seam.

CHAPTER **12** · *Creative Sweatshirts*

Sweatshirts are easy, fast-to-finish projects. What other garment could be serged decoratively in so many different ways? Sweatshirt fabrics are easy to handle and popularly priced! They hold their shape but are flexible enough to "forgive" less-than-perfect serging and fitting.

Don't have time to sew a sweatshirt? Combine decorative threads and stitches to jazz up plain ready-made sweatshirts available in both set-in and raglan sleeves and in a wide range of colors.

The Patterns

All the pattern companies now offer sweatshirt styles for women, men, and kids. Sweatshirt patterns are usually designed with few seams. Unseamed areas on the front and back give you a large area for decorative serging. Even the most basic pullover style can be transformed into a designer sweatshirt.

The Fabric and Ribbing

Sweatshirt fleece can be cotton, cotton/polyester, cotton/acrylic, or 100% polyester. Always preshrink sweatshirt fabrics by washing and drying the fabric **twice** before cutting out. This prevents "progressive" shrinkage. Use laundry detergent to remove any excess sizing and dye.

A wide variety of ribbing is finally available to the homesewer. See pages 98 and 99 for a detailed explanation of types, fibers and sewing techniques and why we **don't** preshrink ribbing.

Thread Possibilities

Because most of us wash rather than dry-clean sweatshirts, decorative threads, yarns and ribbons used should withstand repeated washing and drying. Among the most durable are topstitching thread, crochet cotton, and Woolly Nylon.

Helpful Notions

There are several notions you will find helpful when creatively serging sweatshirts, including a water-soluble marking pen, ruler, and dressmaker's curve, seam sealant like Fray Check® or Fray-No-More,® a seam ripper, and loop turner.

The Stitches

Several decorative stitches are appropriate for sewing creative sweatshirts. Our three favorite stitches for sweatshirts are:

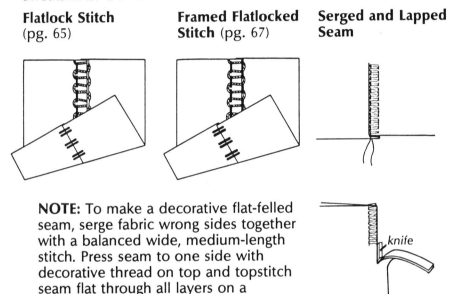

Flatlock Stitch (pg. 65)

Framed Flatlocked Stitch (pg. 67)

Serged and Lapped Seam

NOTE: To make a decorative flat-felled seam, serge fabric wrong sides together with a balanced wide, medium-length stitch. Press seam to one side with decorative thread on top and topstitch seam flat through all layers on a conventional machine.

knife

DECORATIVE SERGING SEWING ORDER FOR RAGLAN SLEEVE SWEATSHIRT

1. Serge all but one back sleeve seam.

2. Add decorative serging. Try one of these ideas:

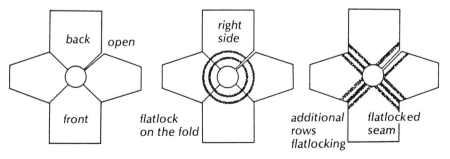

back open

front

right side

flatlock on the fold

additional rows flatlocking

flatlocked seam

3. Then serge ribbing to neckline and sleeves.

4. Serge the back sleeve seam through neck rib.

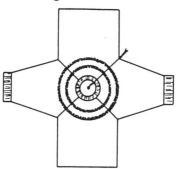

5. Serge one underarm seam.

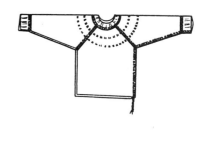

6. Serge the ribbing to the hem.

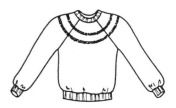

7. Serge other underarm seam.

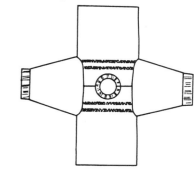

DECORATIVE SERGING SEWING ORDER FOR SET-IN SLEEVE SWEATSHIRT

1. Decoratively serge pieces. Sew one shoulder seam. Apply neck ribbing.

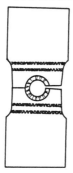

2. Serge other shoulder seam. Set in sleeves. Apply sleeve ribbing.

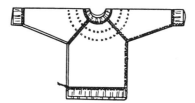

3. Serge one underarm seam. Apply lower ribbing.

4. Serge other underarm seam.

The "Ski Sweater" Sweatshirt

By using your favorite raglan sleeve sweatshirt pattern, you can make a plain sweatshirt into a "ski sweater." A basic ready-made raglan sleeve sweatshirt is also simple to decorate. Consider different colors of thread on the same shirt.

Flatlocked rows.

Flatlocked rows alternating with decorative stitching sewn on a conventional machine.

Flatlocked seams in a color blocked design.

Ribbings attached with decorative flat-felled seams.

MORE CREATIVE IDEAS

Lettuce Edge Ruffling

1. Try on shirt and mark lettuce line first with pins. Then mark line with water-soluble marker.

2. Fold sweatshirt, wrong sides together, on marked line.

3. Stretch folded fabric and serge with a rolled hem stitch. Be careful not to cut the fold.

Fastest Color Splicing Ever

1. Use a striped fabric and flatlock along stripes.

2. **Then** cut out sweatshirt and sew together.

Random Flatlocking

Flatlock stitch at random on fabric before construction.

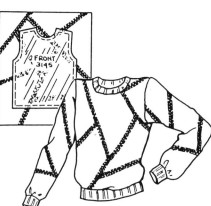

Mock Flatlocked Piecing

Use the same random technique for small areas such as yokes. Flatlock squares. Cut on bias. Mark first with a water-soluble marker.

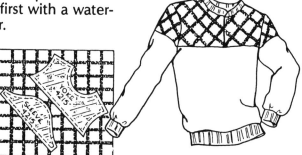

Sensational Serged Sweaters

CHAPTER **13** · *Sensational Serged Sweaters*

Undoubtedly you've admired the gorgeous, spendy sweaters now so popular in ready-to-wear, from casual cardigans to one-of-a-kind hand knit originals. Serging beautifully finishes cut edges, so even hand knits can be "cut and sewn" rather than assembled by hand.

For those without the time or talent to knit, sweaterknit yardage is now more accessible and affordable than ever before. Take an evening to serge a sweater that would surpass any expensive readymade in styling, fit, finishing and durability.

SWEATER KNIT YARDAGE

Once sweater knit yardage was a rare find. Now these factory knitted fabrics are seen in small and large retail stores. Characteristically stable (some are actually double knits), ravel-free, and wide (60" or so), with coordinating ribbing (bands or yardage), these are excellent choices for beginners. Plan on spending more for cotton, wools, and natural fiber blends. More reasonably priced washable acrylics are perfect for kids' clothes and frequently laundered sportswear. If not available locally, try mail order sources. (Most are advertised in **Sew News** and pattern company magazines.)

HAND KNIT OR CROCHET YOUR OWN SWEATER KNIT YARDAGE

For our cut-and-serge method, stick with fine to medium gauge yarns, generally no bulkier than four stitches/inch. Fibers like cotton, wool, linen, acrylic, and blends thereof ravel less than do slippery silks and rayons. After creating the yardage cut out your sweater using a pattern or the tissue from the new McCall's Easy Machine Knitting Patterns.

After knitting, blocking is essential to stabilize and prevent raveling. Blocking is steam pressing the yardage to square it into shape. Follow the yarn label instructions. Generally no additional stabilizing of edges is required before cutting, but if you are unsure, zigzag within the seam allowances before cutting. Or, you can actually stabilize the entire piece with fusible tricot like Easy Knit **before** cutting out.

HOME KNITTING MACHINE YARDAGE

Following the European trend, there's been a resurgence in the popularity of home knitting machines and frames, multiplying sweater knit availability to homesewers.

Inherent advantages of this sweater knit yardage are the custom color/texture combinations, knitting speed, ravel-resistance, and superior stability as compared to hand knits. Also, the fine to medium gauge of most machine knitted sweaterings makes them easy to serge. Best yet, the yarns and ribbons suitable for knitting machines are generally fine and smooth enough for decorative serging. Imagine the coordination possibilities.

Sound interesting? Either knit your own, or contract with a local machine knitter. He or she can assist you in estimating yardage. The width should be a little wider than your widest pattern piece. Be sure to allow this sweater fabric to "relax" after it is taken off the machine. Block before cutting out. Dealers who carry sergers often also sell knitting machines. Take one for a test drive!

WHICH SWEATER KNITS CAN BE SUCCESSFULLY SERGED?

Whether you buy, make or recycle sweater knits, look for these desirable characteristics:

4 or more stitches per inch gauge are easiest to serge

Fine to medium gauge — The finer the gauge, generally the more stable and ravel resistant. A guide for machine and hand knits would be a gauge no larger than 4 stitches per inch. Bulkier sweater knits can be serged successfully, but testing is required.

wrong side

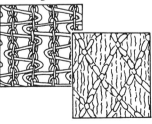

Raschels, other loosely constructed knits or openwork knit laces can present some challenges when serging. They may require slower stitching to prevent catching the fibers on the foot, stitch finger, and/or upper looper.

Yarns that aren't too slippery or nubby — Large slubs or loops can catch on the foot, needle, or upper looper. Silky yarns or ribbons can slip as you serge.

Smooth stitch patterns — Pronounced stitch patterns like cables can be bulky, but usually can be flattened enough with the foot for smooth serging.

CUTTING SWEATER KNITS

Allow 1/2"-1" wide seam allowances. Serging edges can cause what is termed "waves over the ocean" or undesirable stretching. The excess can be trimmed off or finished.

If the ribbing is knitted in, place the sweater hemline at the ribbing edge. Stretch the ribbing to form a straight line. Secure with pins or weights. When the ribbed edge springs back after cutting, it will hug body contours.

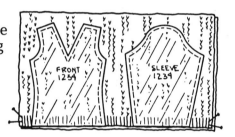

SWEATER KNIT SEAMS

Test, test, test! Never serge along the seam edges. Trim away at least 1/4" to minimize stretching. To decrease bulk at intersecting seams, alternate the direction of the serged seam allowances. The heavier the knit, the wider and longer the stitch should be to prevent waviness. Also, lighten the presser foot pressure for heavier bulkier knits. If the seam is still wavy, ease the fabric with your fingers in front of the presser foot as you sew or serge.

Woolly or stretch nylon thread is a good choice for sweater knits. This soft, yarn-like thread buries itself in the sweater texture, effectively securing the stitches.

Use one of the following to stabilize seams:

Serge over tricot strips —
Sue uses Seams Great® or Seams Saver® on openwork or loosely constructed sweater knits.

lining stabilizer

Use 1″ wide strips of the selvage edge of lining fabrics — Gail's favorite method for shoulder seams. It is soft, non-bulky, and available.

Serge over yarn, ribbon, elastic thread, or cording — Tie a knot at each end to make sure stretch won't occur!

Use a stable stitch

Most stable ←——————————————————→ Stretchier

Sew first with a conventional straight stitch. Then serge seam edges together. This is our favorite for hand and machine knits.	A true 4-thread stitch has little stretch. Use it for shoulders or any seam that requires stabilizing, or where stretch is unnecessary.	A 3/4-thread stitch is nearly as stretchy as a 3-thread and adds a bit more strength to the seam.	A 3-thread stitch has the most give — perfect for sweater knit seams that require stretch, i.e., a turtle neck ribbing seam that will be stretched over the head.	

STABILIZING SWEATER KNIT EDGES FOR SERGING

Stabilizing sweater knit edges will produce more uniform decorative stitches along edges, and prevent unsightly "waves over the ocean" along seams. Stabilize using one of the following:

Fusible tricot like Stacy's Easy Knit® — can be fused to the entire piece or just along seam edges. For less stable hand knits or raschels, Gail likes to fuse with Easy Knit **before** cutting out. On heavier knits, fuse to bodice pieces only. Sleeves can get too bulky.

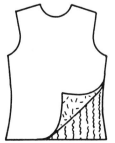

fuse entire piece or . . .

fuse to neckline, armholes, and hem edges

Facings — Select compatible jersey, doubleknit (our dressmaker's choice), or interlock knit to face the edges. Cut the facings according to the pattern, or about 2"-3" wide. Wrong sides together, serge the facings to the garment. Lengthwise grain strips are best for stabilizing straight edges; crosswise or bias are recommended for stabilizing curves.

On sweaterjackets, coats, and other more constructed garments, cut facings to the armhole for extra body. Shoulder pads can be sandwiched between the facing and the sweater knit.

SWEATER DESIGN WORKSHOP

- "Pick up" serged stitches for knitted or crocheted edgings.

- Coordinate buttons and buttonholes with decoratively serged edgings. For matching buttons, wrap a flat, round plastic shank button with the decorative yarn or thread, in an even circular pattern. Dab seam sealant on the wrapping to secure. Continue wrapping until the button is completely covered. Leave a thread tail for sewing the button. Then dab the entire button with seam sealant and allow to dry. The same yarn or decorative thread can be used for handworked buttonholes.

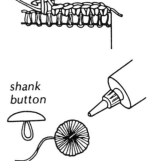

shank button

- Face a sweater knit with a woven fabric. Choose styles with lapels and roll-up cuffs so the lining **will** show! Allow an extra 3/8" on all seams for fitting ease. Wrong sides together, decoratively serge the sweater knit and lining together, using a balanced, decorative stitch.

- Accent sweater knits with lace trim, yardage and appliques. Serged seams "show through" the lace always looking even and trimmed.

14· *Quick Patternless Accessories*

Need an accessory to wear tonight or give tomorrow? Take your pick!! Serging makes them incredibly fast.

FLATLOCKED AND FRINGED ACCESSORIES

Our serger workshop students **love** our scarves and shawls with flatlocked and fringed finishing. See pages 71 and 73 for step-by-step directions.

Experiment with decorative threads, yarns, or ribbons. For heavier fabrics like wools and boucles, consider yarns, pearl cotton, or easy-to-use buttonhole twist/topstitching thread. When flatlocking silks, Gail likes rayon thread or Woolly Nylon.

LARGE SCARF OR SHAWL

Flatlock and fringe all sides with a fringe depth of 1/2".

Suggested fabrics — printed scarf "squares" in rayon or wool challis, silk or silk-like faille, or charmeuse, or lightweight boucles.

40"-60" square yardage required: 40" x 40" size — 1⅛ yard of 45" + fabric. 60" x 60" size 1⅔ yard of 60" width.

MUFFLER

Flatlock and fringe short ends (depth, 1"-3") before finishing long sides with narrow rolled or decorative serging.

Suggested fabrics — light to medium weight wools, wool blends or acrylics (good for sensitive skin!).

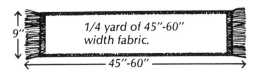

1/4 yard of 45"-60" width fabric.

9"

45"-60"

TIES AND SASHES

Flatlock and fringe short ends before finishing the sides with narrow rolled serging. Braid three ties together for an unusual look.

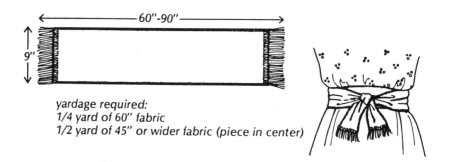

yardage required:
1/4 yard of 60" fabric
1/2 yard of 45" or wider fabric (piece in center)

REVERSIBLES

Line flatlocked and fringed accessories with lighter weight fabric in a contrasting color. Fringe the single layers first. Then place the wrong sides together. For square scarves, straight stitch the two layers together about 1/8" in from the fringing. For oblong mufflers, ties and sashes, fringe the short ends of both layers, then serge the longer edges together using a decorative narrow rolled edge.

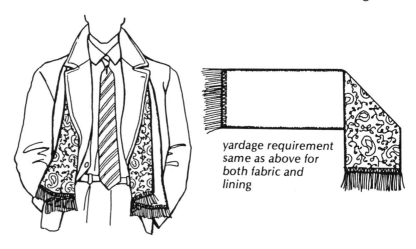

yardage requirement same as above for both fabric and lining

NOTE: See our book, **Sewing With Sergers**, for other scarf sizes and styles.

CHAINSTITCHED AND SERGED BELT

Janet Klaer, of Coats & Clark, showed us a nifty belt that can be sewn entirely on a serger. Use contrasting color lining to create a reversible belt. (You need a serger that will sew a chainstitch.)

Suggested fabrics

Light to medium weight fabrics like linen or linen-likes and silks or silk-likes.

1. Cut two belt pieces, about 3″ wide by your waistline measurement plus 16″. For waist sizes to 29″, 45″ width fabric affords enough length for a belt. For thicker waists, piece with a serged seam to achieve the desired length.

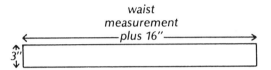

2. Sandwich a layer of polyester fleece between the wrong sides of the fabrics.

3. With a 4/2-thread chainstitch, channel quilt the layers together, alternating stitching direction to prevent grain distortion. To keep rows even, use the presser foot width as the distance between rows. Try using pearl cotton or other decorative thread in the looper and stitch the belt right side down.

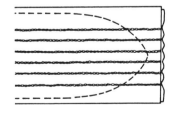

4. Finish the belt edges fast with 2- or 3-thread narrow rolled or balanced serging. If decorative thread was used for chainstitching, use the same thread for the edging and taper the ends.

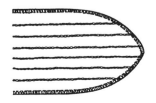

ONE-SIZE-FITS-ALL BELT

1. Cut a strip of synthetic suede like Ultrasuede® Brand Fabric, Facile™, or dressmaker-weight leather. You'll need a piece 1/4 yard wide by at least 44" long. Add body by making the belt double layer. Except for true leathers, you can fuse the layers together with fusible web. One layer can be a contrasting color.

44" or longer

about 4½"

2. Finish the edges with decorative serging.

3. Taper or round off the ends as desired.

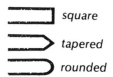

square

tapered

rounded

4. You're almost finished. Thread belt ends through a buckle, one at a time. Adjust to fit.

completed belt
(worn with ends
in or out)

SOFT TOTE IN SECONDS

Finish the edges of three 16" squares with narrow rolled edge serging. Durable, tightly constructed cotton or cotton blend wovens work best.

Straight stitch the scarves right sides together, using a 1/8" wide seam allowance along the serged needle line.

Assemble as shown. Tie the unseamed corners into a square knot.

Great for toting knitting, kids' toys, beach attire or gym clothes!

seams

Serging Specialty Fabrics

The serger can handle nearly every fabric, but some require special handling.

SHEERS AND LACES

Fabrics that are sheer and semi-sheer should be sewn with a narrow serged seam. Because the distance between the needle and knives is always the same it will look totally even in width from the right side. The rolled hem width is particularly invisible from the right side. See page 85.

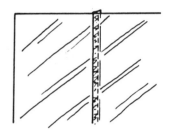

DOTTED SWISS AND EYELETS

Both of these fabrics have raised motifs which can cause irregular serging stitches. This is normal. When finishing with a rolled edge, avoid serging over the raised areas, stitching between the motifs when possible.

VELVETS

For velvets that are thick and ravelly, sew a conventional 5/8" seam and serge the seam allowances single layer to finish. Carefully press the seams open over a velvet pressing board or self fabric.

KNIT OR WOVEN METALLICS

Narrow seams in knitted metallic fabrics will hold up under stress better than in a woven. Test serge a seam in a scrap before beginning project. Serging edges with a matching metallic thread can be sensational. Some metallics may require a serged French seam (see page 124) to prevent the fabric edges from irritating the skin. For rolled edge tips for metallics, see page 86.

QUILTED FABRICS

Two layers of quilted fabrics are sometimes too thick to easily feed into and be
cut by serger knives. The knives only open
about 1/4", so quilted fabrics thicker than
1/4" will bunch up in front of the cutters
and jam.

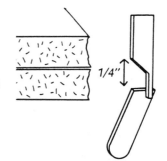

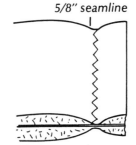

5/8" seamline

To compress quilted fabrics before serging, use a conventional machine to zig-zag
with a long, wide stitch within the seam
allowance next to the seam line. Then
serge directly over the zig-zagging with the
serger needle in the seamline.

For additional strength in quilted
garments that will get lots of wear and
laundering sew a "mock flat felled" seam.
Serge, then press the quilted seam
allowance to one side and topstitch
through all layers on a conventional
machine.

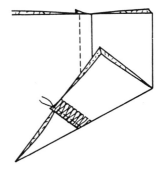

TERRY CLOTH

Terry cloth is a loosely constructed fabric. A serged seam alone will
not be strong enough to withstand stress and repeated launderings.
The following special seam for terry cloth is flat, decorative, strong,
and reversible:

5/8" seamline

1. Serge each single layer with a wide,
   short stitch, trimming away 1/4" of
   the seam allowance.

   NOTE: Make sure the **upper** looper
   thread is on the right side of the
   overlap side and the wrong side of the
   underlap side so seams will be
   reversible.

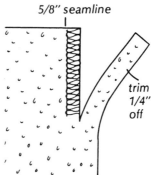

trim
1/4"
off

2. Overlap edges.
Topstitch one edge
through all layers.

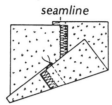

3. Turn over and topstitch
other edge through all
layers.

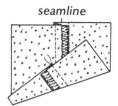

REAL AND FAKE FURS

Fur is too bulky to be sewn with a regular serged seam. Also, the knives would cut the pile. Furs are sewn by professional furriers with a special machine that butts the edges together and sews from one side to the other. We can use a flatlock stitch to simulate the furrier's technique on real and fake furs.

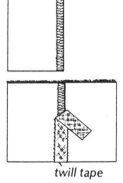

twill tape

1. Trim away the seam allowances. Brush the fur away from the edges toward the right side and place the pieces right sides together. Flatlock.

2. Pull the two pieces to open flat. On the right side, carefully pull out any fur caught in the seam. When working with real fur, reinforce by hand stitching 1/2" twill tape over the seam on the wrong side.

SEQUINED FABRICS

The following tips should help when sewing sequined fabrics:

1. Cut out garment pieces single layer with the pattern on the wrong side of the fabric.
2. Cut through the backing fabric and sequin threads only; avoid cutting sequins. 1" seam allowances are recommended.
3. Carefully unstring sequins from the seam allowances and save.
4. Using a fabric glue like Sobo, secure sequin thread ends to the edge of the seam allowance.
5. Serge seam allowance edges over the sequin thread ends and dried glue. Do not cut away the glue spots.
6. Sew the garment seams on a conventional sewing machine using a zipper foot in order to stitch close to sequins.
7. Carefully press seams open. Test first. Some sequins may discolor or melt with heat.
8. Hand sew leftover sequins to bare spots over the seam line on the right side of the fabric.

CHAPTER 16 · *Lingerie*

Beautiful lingerie is a wonderful addition to any wardrobe and a most welcomed gift. Quickly serged, lingerie sewn at home duplicates the finest readymade underfashions.

THE FABRICS

Cut tricot fabrics with the greatest stretch (usually the crosswise grain) going around the body.

Cut the woven fabrics, like affordable polyester "silkies" or luxurious silks, on the bias. Bias cut woven fabrics allow some "give", but will not stretch as much as a knit. Allow for this when cutting out the garment by using 1"seam allowances for fitting "insurance".

THE SEAMS

NOTE: Use a medium serger stitch length for all the seams. Hold the fabrics taut in front and behind the foot to prevent puckering.

A standard narrow serged seam is an excellent choice for lingerie. Three-thread, 3/4-thread, and 4/2-thread sergers all make a strong, neat lingerie seam.

For a seam without bulk, try a flatlock stitch (see page 66). The seam will lie flat and be inconspicuous under the clingiest skirt or blouse. If using a woven fabric, press under seam allowances before flatlocking.

For a narrow fine seam, use the rolled edge stitch (see page 77), and a 2.5mm length. Because tricots and bias wovens don't ravel, the seam will be strong. Test first. If additional strength is needed, see page 85.

Try "seam locking" with a 2-thread stitch — This is used by some manufacturers.

1. Tighten the needle tension until the needle thread forms a straight line on both sides of the seam.

2. Loosen the looper until the looper thread encases the edge of the fabric. See page 15.

For a durable seam in woven fabrics, try a French seam. It is sewn twice and is very durable, even in loosely constructed fabrics. A French seam is a 3-step process on a conventional machine, but on a serger it is a 2-step process. The following serger instructions are for a 5/8" seam allowance:

1. Set the serger on a 3.5mm stitch width.

2. Place the fabric wrong sides together and serge a seam, allowing the knives to trim away 1/8" of the seam allowance.

3. Press the seam allowance to one side. Press again, encasing the serger seam inside the fabric.

4. On a conventional sewing machine, sew a straight stitch seam 1/4" from the fold (through both layers of fabric), encasing the serger stitch.

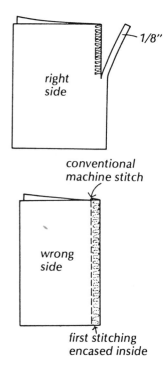

right side

1/8"

conventional machine stitch

wrong side

first stitching encased inside

APPLYING LACES AND TRIMS

Laces and trims can be applied using either a standard serger seam or a flatlock stitch. Stitch all seams with the lace on top so you can see how close the knives trim.

To apply laces and trims with standard serger seams:

1. Place fabric and lace right sides together allowing the fabric to extend approximately 1/8" beyond the edge of the lace. The lace may be taped to the fabric with Scotch® Magic Transparent Tape to prevent slipping.

2. Serge the lace to the fabric, trimming away the extended 1/8" of fabric. Be careful not to cut the lace. By trimming the fabric as the lace is applied, you will not miss the fabric under the lace.

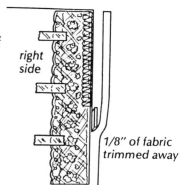

right side

1/8" of fabric trimmed away

3. Press the seam allowance toward the lace so the seam will always lie flat.

To apply laces and trims with flatlocking:

1. Place fabric and lace wrong sides together, allowing the fabric to extend 1/8" beyond the edge of the lace.

2. Flatlock (see page 65) the lace to the fabric trimming away the 1/8" of fabric as you sew.

3. Open and pull the seam flat.

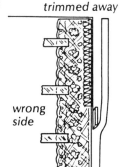

1/8" of fabric trimmed away

wrong side

To apply ribbon and lace simultaneously with flatlocking:

1. Place fabric and lace wrong sides together, with the lace on top. Allow the fabric to extend 1/8" beyond the edge of the lace.

2. Place a narrow (1/16"-1/8") ribbon on top of the lace at the seam edge. Flatlock over the ribbon, encasing it as the lace is serged to the fabric.

3. Open and pull seam flat. The ribbon will be under the flatlocked stitching, on top of the lace.

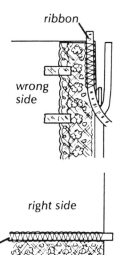

ribbon

wrong side

right side

ribbon

NOTE: The ribbon will stabilize the finished edge, so do not use this accent if the area needs to stretch for wearing ease.

To insert lace with flatlocking:

Insert lace by flatlocking it to the fabric, then trimming away the fabric underneath. Insert the lace before seaming the garment together. This technique is best on a tricot knit.

1. Mark placement lines for lace with a water soluble marker.

2. Center the lace over the placement line on the right side of the fabric.

right side

mark line
placement and
center lace over line

3. Fold the fabric wrong sides together, with the lace on top.

4. Flatlock the lace to the fold being careful not to cut the lace or fabric.

5. Repeat on the other edge of the lace.

6. Open and pull the seams flat.

7. Carefully trim away the fabric under the lace with embroidery scissors.

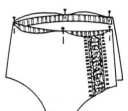

trim fabric from wrong side

APPLYING ELASTIC

Simply quarter the elastic, match to quarter marks on the garment, and stretch to fit as you sew. You may also consider quartering the elastic and the garment again into eighths, to make it even easier to control while serging.

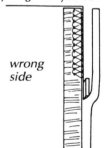

NOTE: You will find it easier to handle the elastic when the garment is flat (before seaming in a circle). To do this, leave a side seam open, apply the elastic and then sew the other side seam. See sewing order on page 128.

1. Place the elastic under the foot, aligning the right edge just to the left of knife. Serge about three stitches into the elastic to secure, stopping with the needle down. Lift the presser foot.

1/8" of fabric to be trimmed by serger as you sew

2. Slip the fabric under the elastic wrong side up. Allow 1/8" of the fabric to extend beyond the edge of the elastic.

wrong side

3. Stretch elastic between marks and serge the elastic to garment, trimming 1/8" of fabric away. Serge SLOWLY, STOPPING WITH THE NEEDLE DOWN WHEN THE ELASTIC NEEDS STRETCHING. Continue to serge until elastic is applied.

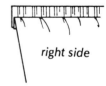

right side

4. Lightly press the seam allowance toward the garment.

Always test a sample of elastic and fabric to check the stitch width and length. A longer than average (about 5mm.) stitch length adjustment will prevent the stitches from bunching together when the elastic relaxes.

ONE-STEP APPLICATION OF LACE TRIM AND ELASTIC

1. See step 1 on page 126.
2. Place the wrong side of the lace on the right side of the fabric. Slip lace and fabric under the elastic. Allow the fabric to extend 1/8" beyond the lace and elastic.
3. Flatlock the lace and elastic to the fabric, stretching the elastic as you sew.
4. Open and pull the seam flat.

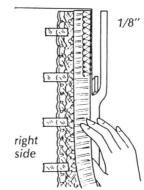

1/8"

right side

LINGERIE STRAPS

Ribbons, lace, and fabric strips make lingerie straps a snap. If color matching ribbons to fabrics is a problem, use strips of the garment fabric to make a quick spaghetti strap (see **Sewing With Sergers**, page 80).

For a quickie strap:

1. Cut 1/4"-1/2" ribbon the finished strap length, plus 2".
2. Cut two pieces of single edge lace trim the same length.
3. Use a flatlock or rolled hem stitch to apply lace to both long edges of the ribbon.

FAST SEWING ORDER FOR CAMISOLE AND TAP PANTS

Create simple elegance on edges of a camisole and tap pants by finishing with a rolled hem (or picot stitch) and rayon, Woolly Nylon, or machine embroidery thread. Variegated shades are lovely.

For Camisole:

1. Serge one side seam.

2. Finish the hem edge and top of bodice with a rolled hem stitch.

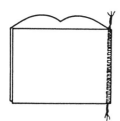

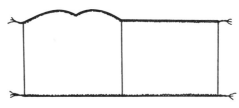

3. Serge the other side seam.

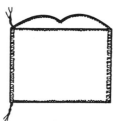

4. Make and apply straps.

For Tap Pants:

1. Serge center front and center back crotch seams.

2. With a rolled hem stitch, serge openings, as shown.

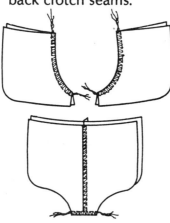

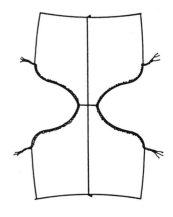

3. Bring the side seam together and serge using the rolled edge stitch.

4. Apply elastic to waist edge before serging the other side seam.

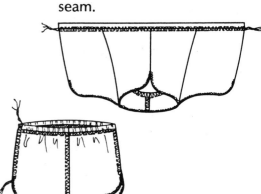

5. Finish the remaining side seam

NOTE: Fast sewing orders for half slips and panties are given in our first book, **Sewing With Sergers.**

Rather than using facings and hems, Sue Green used narrow rolled edge two-thread overedging and variegated thread (in the looper) to finish the edges of this camisole and tap pants. See Chapter 16.

(Above) The most welcomed gift and fastest to make: napkins edge-finished with serging. As a variation, Virginia Fulcher strip-patched the napkins before finishing the edges. See Chapter 19.

(Right) For comfort and the inside-outside look, the serged seams on this baby's leotard were deliberately turned to the outside and topstitched with twin needles. See Chapter 17.

Naomi Baker applied the elastic to the edges of this white engineered print leotard using the casingless method (see Chapter 17). The parallel lines of topstitching were created by straight stitching on a conventional machine with a twin needle. The quick-to-make overskirt is finished with lettuce-leaf edging, easily serged on stretchy knits (see Chapter 17).

CHAPTER 17 · *Creative Aerobic and Swim Wear*

More and more homesewers are serging leotards, tights and swimsuits. The increased interest is no doubt due to the popularity of serging. Our workshop students marvel at serging leotards in an hour or less. After mastering the basics shown in **Sewing With Sergers**, move on to these creative serging ideas.

We like Woolly Nylon or similar brands (see page 25) best for serging aerobic and swimwear because it is very strong and holds the seams well. Plus, it is soft . . . great for body fitting fashions.

INSIDE-OUT FASHION

Aerobic or swim wear can be worn wrong side out! The serged elastic application looks like flatlocking when worn on the outside. All the rage among the Jane Fonda set, these leotards can also be worn right side out for a more traditional look.

Use contrasting thread. Experiment with different stitch widths and lengths . . . generally a medium to wide balanced stitch works best. For more color density, serge again over the first stitching.

For armholes, necklines, and leg openings, serge the raw edges with the contrasting color thread, turn up, and topstitch the elastic casing. Or, use the ready-to-wear technique specially designed by Palmer & Pletsch for McCall's patterns that allows you to serge elastic to the raw edge, then turn up and topstitch. See **Sewing With Sergers** for these complete instructions.

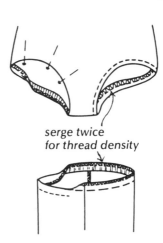

serge twice
for thread density

Serge the side seams with the same contrasting color thread. They become quite narrow in stretchy aerobic wear and look more like a design line.

MORE DESIGN IDEAS

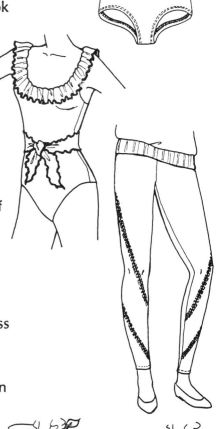

- **Line two-way stretch leotards and swimsuits** with the same fabric in a contrasting color. The additional layer doubles the wearing mileage, smooths the figure, and makes the garment reversible. Sew the fabric and lining separately. Place the two layers wrong sides together and join when applying elastic to the edges.

- **Try a double needle** for topstitching the elastic casing. It is more durable and a great look — often seen in ready-to-wear!

- **Lettuce edge** belts, ruffles, and necklines (page 82).

- **Add ruffles** to a neckline or insert them into a seam. Finish with a rolled edge stitch (see page 77).

- **Color block** or splice tights. Teens love different legs! This look is wild and the price is right; for most, only one yard of fabric is required. Using strong Woolly Nylon thread, flatlock the color spliced seams to minimize bulk.

  NOTE: Another look popular with the aerobic set is stirrupless capri length tights that can also be color blocked. Simply trim the stirrups off and finish the bottom edge with a serged satin stitch.

- **Two-way stretch fabrics make gorgeous pareus.** Buy 1-1/4 yards more of your swimsuit fabric. Finish edges with narrow rolled satin serging. Tie on for an instant dress or skirt, as shown.

AEROBIC HEADBANDS

All exercisers — golfers, tennis players, and joggers — love "sweat" bands. Fishermen and hunters are kept warm with wool headbands. Serge them by the dozen — fast. Use prefinished ribbing, ribbing yardage, or two-way stretch fabrics. Buy fabric or recycle ribbing about 12" long and 2–3" wide (the stretchier, the better). Vary the style with the type of ribbing used.

Two-way stretch fabric headbands

These headbands are in demand for aerobics enthusiasts. They are easy to make because they only require one seam and can double as pull-on belts (for small waists only!). Use cotton/spandex (Lycra®) blend knits for comfort and absorbency.

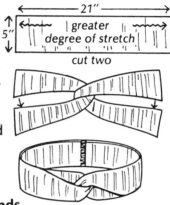

1. Cut two pieces of two-way stretch fabric as shown.

2. Loop the pieces of fabric together. (Don't worry about the raw edges — the knit doesn't ravel and automatically curls under like an instant hem!) Place ends of each loop wrong sides together. Stretch to fit your head and mark seamline.

3. Serge the four layers together.

Medium weight ribbed yardage headbands

1. Fold ribbing in half lengthwise, wrong sides together. Flatlock the seam (see page 65) and pull flat.

2. Stretch it around wearer's head until it is snug, but comfortable. Mark seamline and serge.

Variation: Add a twist before seaming, as shown.

Medium to heavy ribbed band headbands

NOTE: This type of ribbing has one finished edge.

1. Cut a single layer and finish the one raw edge with medium to wide balanced serging. Trim at least 1/4" off the raw edge while serging to prevent stretching.

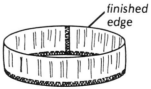

2. Stretch to fit head, mark seamline and serge.

CHAPTER **18 •** *Creative Ideas for Children*

When it comes to kids' clothes, sergers are indispensable. Finally, you'll sew fast enough to keep up with those fast growing bodies.

The childrenswear you serge instantly (well, almost!) will look better and last longer than any ready-mades. Both Pati (daughter, Melissa) and Gail (daughter, Bett) have noticed that their serged "custom-mades" stand up to repeated washings!

SERGER SHORTCUTS

Replace bindings — on jackets and vests with decorative serging. If the garment is reversible, use a stitch that looks the same, or is decorative, on the upper and lower looper.

Create your own trim — the cost savings are substantial. Finish one or both of the edges with a narrow rolled edge. If there is enough fabric, cut the fabric strips on the bias for softness and stitch uniformity. For ruffles, gather on a conventional sewing machine (we like special ruffler attachments or gathering feet).

Shirr with serging. Thank goodness Sue Green developed this technique — it's the only shirring Pati or Gail have time to finish. Shirr the fabric before cutting out the garment. (See page 70.)

Make frilly blouses and dresses fast!
Pin tucks are perfect. Experiment with fine shiny threads like rayon and different stitch lengths.

1. Tuck the fabric before cutting out.

2. Press mark the tuck fold lines.

3. Plan serging direction so the top side of the stitch will always show on the right side.

4. Disengage knife, if possible.

5. Serge along the foldline with a narrow rolled edge or a narrow balanced stitch.

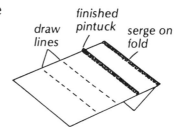

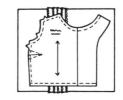

draw lines   finished pintuck   serge on fold

QUICK-TO-SERGE KIDSWEAR IDEAS

Serge children's swimwear, leotards and tights. Chances are if you've sewn your own, there will be enough yardage left over for a wee one. (See page 130.)

Serge Halloween get-ups! Buy preprinted costumes that glow in the dark. No more facings or bindings. Anxious Halloween goblins love the super-fast process.

Serge reversibles. Simple silhouettes like tee-shirts and jumpers are perfect candidates. (See page 102.)

BABY'S BOUNTY

Serged diapers! Choose super absorbent 100% cotton terry (preferred in England where they're called "nappies"), special diaper flannel, or knits. Simply serge finish the edges. Use two to four layers, depending on the fabric weight.

Sizes: 11" x 13 1/2" for infants to nine months. 13 1/2" x 16 1/2" for toddlers.

As a starter set, most babies need at least three dozen or about 2 1/2 yards of 45" fabric for infants and 5 3/4 yards of 45" fabric for toddlers.

Serge blankets! Look for 100% cotton flannel or soft acrylic sweaterknits. An ample size is 45" x 45" or 1 1/4 yard of 45" width fabric. For newborn babies, 30" x 40" receiving blankets are nice. Make them double if using flannel. Finish the edges with baby yarn in the upper looper. Or use #8 pearl cotton in both upper and lower loopers.

Blanket variations!

Add a protective hood to one corner. When made in terry cloth, this is the perfect after-bath "robe".

Flatlock satin blanket binding or ribbon to the edges. Pati's new daughter Melissa has adopted a satin-edged blanket as her favorite.

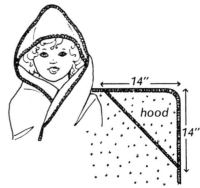

Make our favorite no-tie bib.
You'll need one fringed guest towel about 11" x 18" and 2" wide cotton or cotton blend ribbing that is about 16" in length.

1. Fold the guest towel as shown. Trim out the neckline opening using a large cereal bowl as a guide.

2. Cut the ribbing 4"-5" shorter than the neckline edge measurement but large enough to fit over the child's head (See page 100).

3. Seam the ribbing and serge to the neckline, evenly distributing the ease (See page 100).

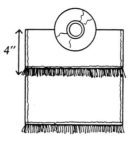

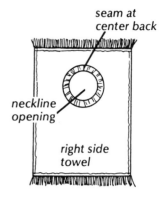

seam at center back

neckline opening

right side towel

CHAPTER **19** • *Home Decorating and Crafts*

No time to sew? Satisfy your creative urges and make your home more beautiful with these super-fast-to-serge projects.

NAPKINS

Somehow **cloth** napkins transform any meal into a dining occasion. Plus, serging napkins is a productive way to perfect decorative stitching, particularly the rolled edge. Gail's **first** serger project was 75 napkins. . . .every one was serged with a different tension!

There's not an easier to make nor more welcomed gift than cloth napkins. Dive into your fabric stash . . . good chance there's a cotton or cotton blend perfect for napkins. Unlike 100% synthetic readymades (Pati's pet peeve) they'll really absorb!

Yardage Estimates

	Quantity	Fabric Widths 45"	54"
18" x 18" (dinner size)	Four	1 yard	1 yard
	Six	1½ yards	1 yard
	Eight	2 yards	1½ yards
15" x 15" (size of most readymades and the most economical to make from 45" width fabric)	Four	7/8 yard	7/8 yard
	Six	1⅜ yards	7/8 yard
	Eight	1⅜ yards	1⅜ yards

Serging Tips

- Chain off at corners. It's the fastest and easiest method. Serge finish lengthwise grain edges first, then the crosswise grain. The lengthwise grain has less tendency to pull out at the corners where the edge finishing intersects. Dab Fray Check® or Fray-No-More® on corners. Allow to dry, then snip.
  We know a restaurant owner who has her 400 home-serged napkins laundered and pressed daily. After a year, she hasn't detected noticeable fraying at the corners. To avoid dog-eared corners, see page 87.

- Experiment with thread types. Woolly Nylon is our favorite choice because it spreads to cover a rolled edge beautifully, and minimizes fraying at the corners. Other thread types we like for finishing include: cotton covered polyester; buttonhole twist; rayon thread, especially variegated; metallics for holiday table toppings; or two strands of all-purpose or serger thread.

- Experiment with stitch types. Although a rolled edge (see pages 8-87) remains the most popular and durable finish for cloth napkins, a balanced stitch is a refreshing look. Use buttonhole twist in both the upper and lower loopers.

Creative Ideas

- Line with coordinating or contrasting fabric. Serge edge finish as one layer. Lining is a clever way to tie together related, but not matching, prints and colors. Many of our workshop students like to work with self-fabric so that the wrong side of a print won't show.

  Also, to strengthen edges, align crosswise and lengthwise edges. Rolled edges will be more uniform on all four sides, too.

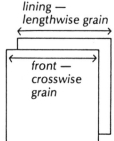

- Make strip patchwork napkins. Serge the strips together, then straight stitch the longest strip to the napkin, right sides together, as shown. Fold the strip triangle down, enclosing the seams. Serge finish the napkin edges.

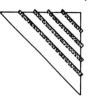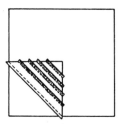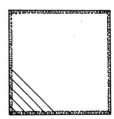

- Have fun folding cloth napkins — even kids love to do it!

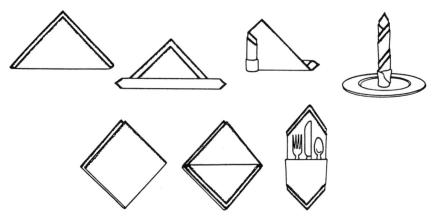

PLACEMATS

Placemats are handy for everyday use and a snap to serge! Make a set to match your napkins. Only one yard of 45" wide fabric will yield six 14" by 16" placemats. Use your favorite readymade placemat as a pattern.

Yardage estimates — Yardages are given for single thickness only and for 14" by 16" size. Double the yardage for reversible or lined placemats.

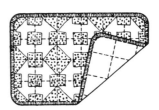

Quantity	Fabric Widths	
	45"	54"
Four	1 yard	1 yard
Six	1 yard	1 yard
Eight	2 yards	1½ yards

Fabric tips — Use double-sided quilted fabric for super-quick placemats. Just serge the edges and you're done! For firmer placemats, try these layering strategies:

Single-sided quilted fabric **plus** fusible web **plus** single-sided quilted fabric.

Single-sided quilted fabric **plus** fusible web **plus** fabric.

Fabric **plus** batting **plus** fabric with fusible web between the layers.

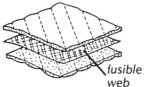

fusible web

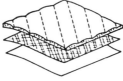

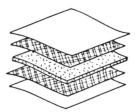

All the above may be channel quilted with conventional straight stitching.

NOTE: For batting, we like bonded fiberfill like Stacy's Thermo Lam® or Pellon® Fleece.

Serging tips — Facilitate continuous serging by rounding off corners. Use a cup as a template. Trim with a rotary cutter. Or cut placemats in an oval shape.

If batting-filled placemats are too thick to feed into the knives smoothly, compress the layers first with a wide, long conventional zigzag, then serge edge finish.

Use the "belly button" rule —
start serging in the center of the
bottom edge of the placemat. Less-
than-perfect lapping of the serging
will be hidden under the dinner plate!

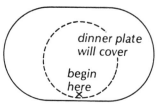

If you can't use a heavy thread
in the lower looper, yet want the
placemats to be reversible, wrap the
edge. See page 42.

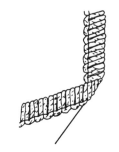

Make flatlocked and fringed
placemats (see page 72). Choose
loosely woven linen looks and put
your television watching troops to
work fringing!

Thread types — Experiment with different threads. On heavier,
multi-layer or quilted and stitched placemats, we like heavier
threads such as pearl or crochet cotton or topstitching thread used
in both loopers with a wide, balanced stitch. On thinner, single layer
placemats, try Woolly Nylon, all-purpose, and rayon threads in a
medium width balanced stitch. A rolled edge can also be used, giv-
ing a unique look to lightweight placemats.

PILLOWS

Make tie-ons for square
pillows. The tie-ons should
be twice the pillow size
(e.g., a 16" pillow requires
two 32" squares). Roll the
edges of the squares and
tie on, gathering the fabric
into attractive folds. For
smaller squares, simply
hand tack corners to pillow.
Great for pre-printed motifs.

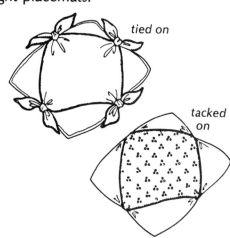

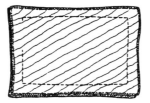

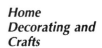

Finish ruffles with rolled edge. For extra body, make ruffles double layer using self-fabric or a contrasting color.

Make instant pillows! Serge edges of each piece separately, then straight stitch together 2" from edge for a flanged look. Leave a 4" opening for stuffing.

Flatlock fringe squares of fabric. Stitch together leaving a 4" opening for stuffing.

QUILTS AND CRAFTS

A version of vintage "crazy quilts" — flatlocked patchwork simulates hand worked feather embroidery stitches. Topstitching thread, fine yarn and pearl cotton are recommended. Block quilts are easiest and fastest.

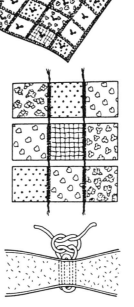

1. Plot the patchwork color scheme.

2. Flatlock all parallel rows in one direction. (It may be necessary to compress layers first with a wide, long zig-zag stitch.)

3. Chain between blocks as shown. Then flatlock all rows in the opposite direction, trimming off the chains between rows.

4. Tuft through all layers and edge finish with decorative serging.

Use your quilted fabric for quilts, handbags, garments, doll accessories, and pillows. Let your imagination go!

Transform your serger into a stripping machine! — Remove the needles and thread. Mark the desired width from the knife on the front guard plate. Align the fabric edge with this mark as you feed fabric through serger to cut strips. This stripping method is a welcome relief for hands tired from cutting yards and yards of rag baskets, rag knitting, "rag point" and braided rugs.

CHAPTER 20 • *The Serger Challenge*

The serger has been popular in home sewing only for a few years. Most of us use it in a straightforward way, to make seams or to decorate edges. But we suspect the capabilities of this handy little machine have barely been tapped.

Now that you've worked your way through the book, learning to change decorative threads, stitch width and length, needle and looper tensions, we challenge you to extend the frontiers of the serger. What techniques and effects can you develop using the serger as a creative tool?

This chapter shows you a few samples by artists who have been playing with their machines. We hope it will spark your own experiments. On page 145 is a worksheet you can photocopy onto postcard stock, to help you keep track. Remember, artists make masses of small samples, most of which are "failures." Seeing what doesn't work, however, is an integral part of seeing what does.

PLAY WITH THE LINE

Lois Ericson is a designer, teacher, and author from Tahoe City, CA. The photos on this page and the next two are from her new book *TexTure/A Closer Look* (200 pages, 16 pages color, $21.95 from PO Box 1680-CSI, Tahoe City, CA 95730). Here Lois has played with undulating curves, which are worked separately and then sewn with a conventional sewing machine to a backing.

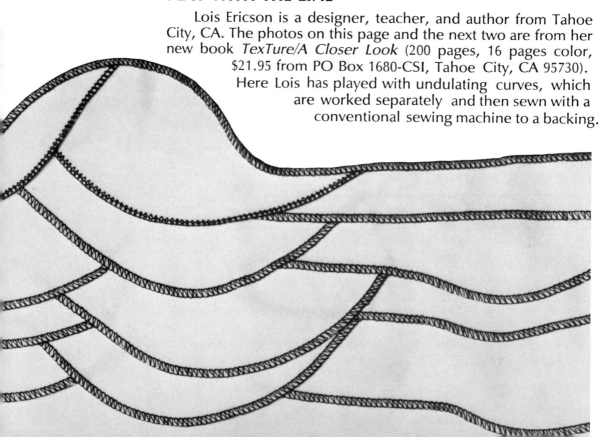

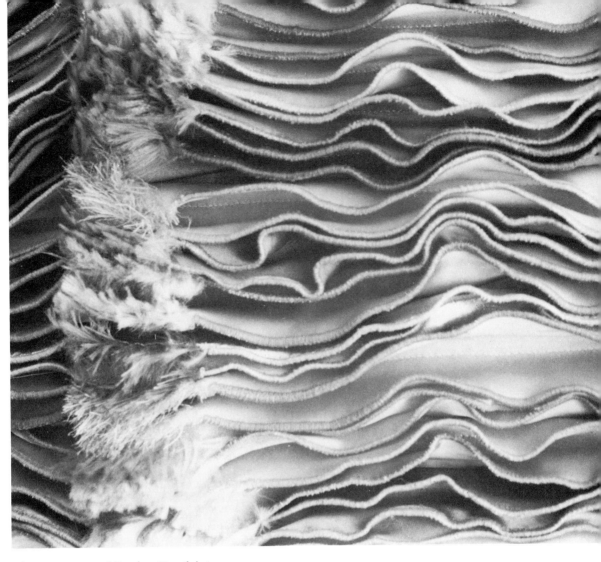

(photo courtesy of Emelyn Garofolo)

PLAY WITH THE TEXTURE

Emelyn Garofolo, a designer from Copiague, New York, calls this technique "Idiot's Delight." She cuts strips of woven fabric on the bias, then satin stitches the edge twice ("but I'm going to try this with a rolled edge on a serger," she says). In the unworked area, she frays the threads.

What if you serged two different types of woven fabric together—shiny and matte, for example? What would the fringe look like? What if you serged two contrasting colors together?

PLAY WITH THE FABRIC'S CHARACTERISTICS

Emelyn Garofolo was working on a piece using the "Idiot's Delight" technique (see previous page), for which she needed brown fabric. All she could find was a piece of brown knit. When she tried to satin stitch it, "the brown knit had a mind of its own." The fabric began to flute and ruffle. Rather than throw it away and search for a different brown fabric, Emelyn thought, "This has great potential for exploring."

Later she came up with this piece, which uses fabric salvaged from sweaters. She satin stitched the raw edges together, stretching it more or less, according to how much fluting she wanted. Then she sewed the fabric into tubes and top-stitched it onto a fabric background.

Think of other fabric characteristics: the moldability of wool, the wrinkling of linen, the drape of silk, the fraying of cotton. How can you use your machine to exploit these characteristics?

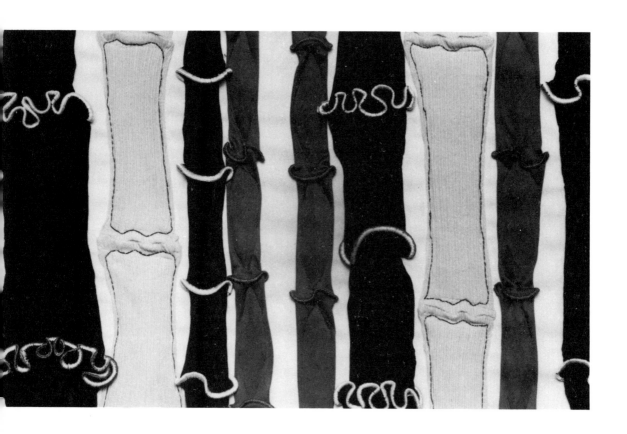

PLAY WITH A TECHNIQUE

What other needlework techniques can you translate to serging—quilting, knitting, cross-stitch, beading? Here we've put a rolled edge on both sides of 2"-wide strips, taken a tuck at each short end, and woven the strips. If you used a shiny fabric like silk, the play of light would make a rich surface. Or you could keep the fabric plain and play with the color of the thread edge, using different colors or a variegated thread. Lois Ericson made a vest using this serged-edge weaving technique, padding the inside with a light batting.

Could you gather one fabric to another with the serger elastic foot and stuff the space between with batting?

Could you make an old-fashioned biscuit quilt completely by serger?

Could you make a decorative thread tail several yards long using pearl cotton in the loopers and then couch it with a regular sewing machine in an African design on a caftan?

What will you dream up?

(sample worked by Robbie Fanning)

MANIPULATE THE EDGE

After you've serged a fabric, play with manipulating the edge: cut it up, shirr it, tuck it, fold it. Here, adapting an idea from Gunnar Sundstrom of Palm Bay, FL, we've serged the edges of 2"-wide fabric with two colors of pearl cotton in the upper and lower loopers. These were then serged across, making 2" squares. The points were sealed with seam sealant and the squares folded into triangles. These triangles were stitched down their centers with a sewing machine onto a backing fabric.

You will need to keep track of your settings for all of these experiments, so we've designed a worksheet on the next page for you to photocopy.

Have fun!

(sample by Robbie Fanning)

WORKSHEET—CREATIVE SERGING *ILLUSTRATED*
(Photocopy this page onto postcard stock.)

Date:

Design inspiration:

Idea:

Fabric:

Evaluation:

NOTES:	THREAD	TENSIONS				STITCH	
		NEEDLE(S)		LOOPER(S)			
		LN	RN	UL	LL	Length	Width

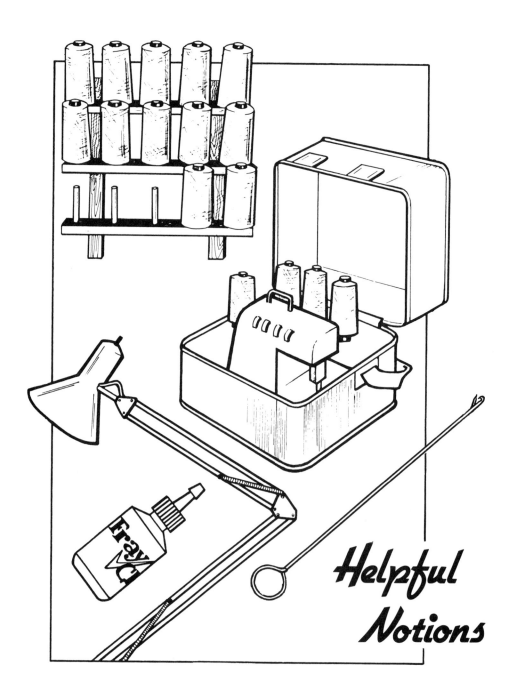

Helpful Notions

Helpful Notions

Some of these notions come with your serger, but all of them can be purchased separately. Here's what they're used for:

Auxiliary Lights
For more light! Some fasten directly to the serger. Also available are flexible arm lights that fasten to the table.

Basting Tape
Regular and water-soluble basting tapes hold fabrics like slinky, silk-likes in place while serging.

Compressed Air
Keeps your serger lint-free!

Extension Table
Creates a flat surface around the serging area.

Glue Stick
Temporarily bastes seams and trims for easier serging. Washable.

Lint Brush
For quick cleaning of small areas.

Loop Turner
For burying thread tails under serging.

Magnetic Seam Guide
Attaches to the knife cover as a guide for accurate serging. Movable to trim various widths.

Magnifying Lens
Attaches to the front of your serger for magnifying threading and stitching.

Needle and Looper Threader
Assists in threading needle(s) and looper(s).

Needle Nose Pliers or Needle Grippers
For easy, straight insertion of serger needles.

Needles for Sergers
Have lots of sizes for your serger on hand. Your serger can be damaged if the wrong type of needle is used. See your manual or ask your dealer.

Rotary Cutter and Cutting Mat
Cut out fast! Both available in a variety of sizes.

Screw Driver
For changing needles, knives, and on some sergers, stitch settings. Standard equipment with most sergers but replacement sizes are available.

Seam Ripper
Rip any serged seam quickly!

Seam Sealant
Liquid plastic like Fray Check® and Fray-No-More® that secures stitches. Super for corners.

Serger Knives
Work together to trim the fabric. Replacement for the softer knife comes with your serger, or can be purchased, as can the more expensive steel alloy knife.

Serger Foot Pedal Mat
Slotted rubber mat prevents pedal from sliding.

Thread Nets
Prevent slippery threads from dropping off the spool or cone while serging.

Thread Racks
For neat, compact storage of coned and tubed threads!

Tote Bags
Indispensable for care-free transporting. Not a standard serger accessory. Both hard and soft carrying cases available.

Washable Markers
Substitute for notches when serging. Either water- or air-erasable.

Troubleshooting

Problem	Solution
• **Skipped Stitches**	• Replace a bent, dull or damaged needle. • Use a needle the correct size for the fabric and thread. • Thread correctly, through all guides and eyes. Thread can easily come out of the open thread guides. The looper **or** needle tension may be too tight. Loosen one then the other to see which works. • Change needle size. • Insert needle correctly. The eye of the needle must face **exactly** toward the front of the machine. • Increase the presser foot pressure for heavier fabrics.
• **Puckered Fabric**	• Loosen needle thread tension. • Adjust foot pressure. • Check for correct threading. • Shorten the stitch length. • Check for correct cutting from the knives.
• **Excessive Stretching**	• Lighten the foot pressure. • Lengthen stitch. • Stabilize edge (see page 56) • Serge in from the edge, trimming off at least 1/4". • Be careful not to stretch fabric as you sew.
• **Irregular Stitches**	• Thread correctly. • Replace with a new or different size needle. • Insert needle correctly. • Adjust tension. • Change to the correct size needle for thread or fabric. • Thread must feed from the spool smoothly. • Check for proper cutting action of knives. **NOTE:** If the texture of the fabric is uneven, irregular stitches will occur. It is difficult to compensate for this.
• **Fabric Doesn't Feed Well**	• Presser foot is up. • Lengthen the stitch. • Increase or decrease foot pressure depending on fabric weight. • Clean lint out of feed dogs. • Check knife blades for excessive wear.
• **Thread is Breaking**	• Check for thread caught on spool notch, thread stand or guides on machine. • Rethread machine in proper threading order. • Balance the tension settings. • Insert needle correctly. • Loosen tension on the breaking thread. • Change the needle. • Use a high-quality thread.

Problem	Solution
● **Needle Breaks**	● Change to a new needle. ● Insert the needle correctly. ● Change to a larger size needle. ● Check for thread caught or trapped in a thread guide. ● AVOID EXCESSIVE PULLING OF THE FABRIC WHILE SERGING.
● **Machine Jams**	● Pull thread tails to the back as you begin to serge. ● Make sure fabric trimmings fall away from, not into, the serger. ● Lengthen stitch, especially if using heavy threads. ● Close protective front cover while serging. ● Serge fewer layers of fabric or compress thick layers. ● Check for proper cutting position of knives.
● **Seam Pulls Open to Expose Stitches**	● Tighten the needle tension, or ● Loosen the lower looper tension. ● Check to see if thread is engaged in the tension dials.
● **Excessive Machine Noise**	● Clean and oil machine. ● Insert new needle. ● Check alignment of knife blades. ● Consult your dealer if problem persists. **NOTE:** Check to see if the surface that the machine is sitting on is making the noise.
● **Trimmed Edge is Ragged**	● Reset knife blades correctly. ● Change to a new blade. ● Allow machine to trim at least 1/8″ off the fabric edge.

SELECTING THE PROPER WIDTH, LENGTH AND NEEDLE SIZE

Weight	Fabric Type	Width	Length	Needle Size
Light	Voile	2.5mm	2.0mm	12 (80)
	Gingham	3.5mm	2.5mm	12
	Georgette	1.5mm*	2.5mm	12
	Sheer	1.5mm*	2.5mm	12
	Lace	1.5mm*	2.0mm	12
	Silk & Silkies	2.5mm	2.5mm	12
Medium Woven	Poplin	4.0mm	3.0mm	12-14 (80 or 90)
	Gabardine	4.0mm	3.0mm	12-14
Medium Knit	Jersey	4.0mm	2.0mm	12-14
	T-shirting	4.0mm	2.0mm	12-14
	Double Knit	4.0mm	2.0mm	12-14
Heavy	Denim	5.0mm	2.0mm	14-16 (90 or 100)
	Terry Cloth	5.0mm	2.0mm	14-16
	Corduroy	5.0mm	2.5mm	14-16
	Velour	5.0mm	2.5mm	14-16
	Wools	4.5mm	3.0mm	12-14

*Rolled hem width.

LOVE AND CARE OF YOUR SERGER

Keep It Clean

Lint quickly builds up under the throat plate and can clog knife blades, causing skipped stitches. If lint builds up on the thread guides, it can cause uneven threads feeding through the machine. Dust often with the soft brushes supplied with your machine or use canned compressed air. Attach the straw-like tube to the nozzle for the most powerful spraying action.

Oil as Necessary

Use an oil specially made for sergers. Check your manual for oiling points. Many machines need to be oiled after 8-10 hours of high speed serging. If your machine is making more noise than usual, it likely needs oil.

Change Needles

Needles with sharp, smooth points are essential to care-free serging. If the needle is slightly dull or burred, it will cause a clicking noise and possibly skipped stitches. Synthetic fibers dull needles more quickly than natural fibers. Change the needle when skipped or irregular stitches occur. Sometimes changing to a different **size** needle improves stitching quality.

Change the Knife Blades

If you avoid cutting pins, your knives last much longer. When the trimmed edge is ragged, however, one or both blades may be dull. One is made of hard alloy steel and rarely needs changing. The other is softer so is usually the only one that will be dull or damaged. Thick fabrics and synthetics also dull blades faster. Check your manual to see which of the blades on your serger is the softer one (it will be the least expensive). **Replace** a dull blade, being sure it is inserted properly.

NOTE: Serger knives cannot be resharpened like scissors with a "knife" edge. They cut because of the downward force of the two rectangular edges coming together.

FIT BEFORE YOU SERGE

Once serged, a seam cannot be let out. Hence, it is imperative that you fit before you serge. Pin fitting the pattern is fast and approximates fit amazingly well. However, if you've never used a pattern before, are uncertain about the amount of ease allowed and have a poor track record when it comes to fit, *measure*. Compare your measurements to the patterns, then alter accordingly. Allowing at least 1" seam allowances can't hurt; this fitting insurance compensates for inaccurate measuring and weight gains.

The following guidelines to comfort ease should help you determine whether your pattern will fit. "Comfort ease" is the minimum amount of ease required to reach, sit, walk and drive comfortably. There are, however, exceptions to these basic ease guidelines. Knits generally require less ease (although sweatshirts have been oversized lately). An authentic jean fit is skin tight, with little or no hip or crotch ease.

COMFORT EASE CHART (FOR MEN AND WOMEN)

Garment	Bust/Chest*	Hip*	Sleeve Girth*
Swim/Aerobicwear	(less**)	(less**)	(less**)
Dresses	2½"	2½"	2½"
Jackets	4"	4"	4½"
Coats	5"	5"	5½"
Trousers	—	3"	—
Jeans	—	0	—

*Measure at the fullest part of the bust/chest, hip or sleeve girth.

**Because two-way stretch fabrics with at least 50% stretch are used for these garments, fit can be "under body," or less than the body measurements. Pattern guide sheets explain how to alter when using these fabrics.

This chart is adapted from *Painless Sewing* (revised edition), Palmer/Pletsch Associates (PO Box 12046, Portland, OR 97212-0046), 1986, $7.95 postpaid.

FOR YOUR HEIRS

You spent a lot of time deciding which serger to buy and learning its capabilities. Why not share that wealth of information with the people who will inherit your machine? Besides, each machine has its own quirks. For example, the setting for rolled edge on your machine may be different from the setting on someone else's identical model. Make it easier on your heirs. Record your machine's vital statistics below.

Brand and model _____

Date purchased _____

Cost _____

Vendor name and address _____

Length of warranty _____

Warranty notice and sales slip stored where? _____

Type of machine (2-thread, 3-thread, etc.) _____

Width of stitch(es) _____

Distance of knife from needle(s) _____

Extra accessories _____

Best settings* _____

    regular seam _____

    flatlock _____

    rolled edge _____

    decorative serging _____

        topstitching thread _____

        pearl cotton _____

        fine yarn _____

*These settings change according to thread and fabric, but here's a start. Remember: always test!

MAIL ORDER INFORMATION

Serger Brands and Manufacturers

Addresses are listed on the copyright page. Write the companies for current model specifications and dealer referrals. Many firms will also sell videos, manuals, serger workbooks directly.

Serger Notions, Accessories, and Thread Sources

Aardvark Adventures in Crafts
Box 2449
Livermore, CA 94550
Specialty threads and creative information. Sample issue, $1.00.

Catherine's
Rt. 6, Box 1227
Lexington, NC 27292
Serger parts, threads, books, videos. For info, thread color card, send $1 and a business-sized SASE with $.39 postage.

Clotilde, Inc.
237 SW 28th St.
Ft. Lauderdale, FL 33315
Serger threads, needles, notions. Catalog, $1.00.

D&E Distributing
199 N. El Camino Real #F-242
Encinitas, CA 92024
Decorative threads. Send business-sized SASE.

Home-Makers Supply Co.
2300 NE Broadway
Portland, OR 97232
Coned threads. SASE for price list.

Home-Sew
Bethlehem, PA 18108
Serger needles, threads, notions. Free catalog.

Horn of America
800 Virginia Ave Plaza, Ste 53
Ft. Pierce, FL 33482
Cabinets and tables for sergers. Catalog, $1.00 (indicate interest in serger-related products).

Nancy's Notions
PO Box 683
Beaver Dam, WI 53916
Complete selection of threads, accessories, needles, books, videos. Catalog, $1.00.

National Thread and Supply
695 Oak Rd
Stockbridge, GA 30281
Serger threads, on cones. Free catalog.

Newark Dressmaker Supply
6473 Ruch Rd
Lehigh Valley, PA 18001
Serger threads, needles, books. Free catalog.

Oregon Tailor Supply
2123A Division St
Portland, OR 97202
Serger threads on commercial yardage cones. Business-sized SASE with $.39 postage for price list.

Perfect Notion
566 Hoyt St
Darien, CT 06820
Serger threads, carrying cases, notions, books. Free catalog ($1.00 for first-class postage).

Porcupine Pincushion
PO Box 1083
McMurray, PA 15317
Notions. Free catalog.

Serging Ahead
PO Box 45
Grandview, MO 64030
Serger supplies, books, patterns. Catalog, $1.00.

Sergemate
PO Box 67023
Houston, TX 77067
Table-top work surface accessory for sergers. SASE for free info.

Sew-Art International
PO Box 550
Bountiful, UT 84010
Decorative threads, notions, accessories. Also creative sewing seminars. Free information

Sewing Emporium
1987 Third Ave
Chula Vista, CA 92010
Wide variety of serger needles, parts, threads, accessories. 112-page catalog, $2.00.

Sew-Fit Co.
PO Box 565
LaGrange, IL 60525
Coned threads. Free information.

Speed Stitch
3113-D Broadpoint Dr
Harbor Heights, FL 33950
All-purpose, decorative and specialty serging threads, some books and accessories. Catalog, $3 (whsle and rtl)

Threads West
430 East State St
Redlands, CA 92373
Coned thread (to 12,0000 yard cones), serger parts and accessories for every brand/model. Free color list--include business-sized SASE and your serger brand/model number.

Treadleart
25834 Narbonne Ave, Ste I
Lomita, CA 90717

Books, supplies, notions, decorative threads, and creative inspiration. Catalog, $1.00. Also publishes magazine.

T-Rific Products Co
PO Box 911
Winchester, OR 97495
Polyester serger thread. Color chart, $1.25.

Trovato Sewing Catalog
1741 First Ave South
Seattle, WA 98134
Polyester and cotton-coned threads. Catalog, $1.00.

Tucker Enterprises
5545 Harlan
Arvada, CO
Thread rack for spools and cones. Brochure and prices, business-sized SASE.

YLI Corporation
45 West 300 North
Provo, UT 84601
Threads galore. Specialty, all-purpose and decorative threads, most on cones. Serger yarns and ribbons. Catalog, $1.50.

Aerobic/Swimwear Fabric Sources

Green Pepper, Inc.
941 Olive St
Eugene, OR 97401
Nylon and Lycra blend knits, plus aerobic and cycling wear patterns. Catalog, $1.00.

Jehlor Fantasy Fabrics
17900 Southcenter Parkway, Ste 290
Seattle, WA 98188
Hard-to-find heavyweight Lycra blend fabrics for dancing and skating, and weights suitable for exercising and swimming. Specialty patterns too. Catalog, $2.50.

Keiffers
1625 Hennepin Ave
Minneapolis, MN 55403
Nylon and cotton Lycra blend knits. Discount prices and sales. Free catalog.

Heirloom Serging Fabric and Lace Sources

Donna Lee's Sewing Center
25234 Pacific Hwy South
Kent, WA 98032
Batiste, laces, embroideries, entredeuxs, threads, all fine quality. Catalog, $3.00.

Lacis
2990 Adeline
Berkeley, CA 94703
New and antique laces, in a wide variety. Lace catalog, $1.50.

Seminars/Workshops

Palmer/Pletsch Workshops are held in selected sites across the US and Canada. For information, write Palmer/Pletsch Workshops, P.O. Box 12046, Portland, OR 97212.

Other Serger References

Function and Fashion videotape, produced by the Tacony Corporation and starring Nancy Nix. Serger tips demonstrated on Baby Lock models. Available where Baby Locks are sold or write the company c/o Baby Lock USA, Box 2634-CSI, St. Louis, MO 63116.

McCall's Focus on Overlock Sewing by Gail Brown and Pati Palmer, McCall's Pattern Company (230 Park Ave, New York, NY 10169), 1987. $1.00 postpaid.

Overlock Sewing, A Guide for Using Overlock Sewing Machines by Coats and Clark, Inc. (Box 1010, Toccoa, GA 30577), 1985. $2.50 postpaid.

Palmer/Pletsch Teaching Aids includes eight 22-1/2" x 24" posters illustrating serger tension adjustments. $27.00 postpaid from PO Box 12046, Portland, OR 97212-0046.

Serge and Sew, Timesaving Serger Tips; Serge-A-Quilt; Sew Intimate, all by Ann Person, Stretch and Sew, Inc. (PO Box 185, Eugene, OR 97440), 1984, 1985, 1986 respectively. Available at stores that carry Stretch and Sew products and patterns or by writing the company.

Serger Construction Methods and Serger Principles by Barbara Morales and Ernestine Porter, USDA (University of Idaho, Moscow, ID 83843), 1985. $.80 postpaid for both brochures. Also ask about videos.

Serger/Overlock Sewing I and II, featuring Nancy Zieman, hostess of the *Sewing with Nancy* cable TV series. Recommended 60-minute videotapes that include basic and decorative serging how-tos. Complete descriptions in $1.00 catalog from Nancy's Notions, PO Box 583-CSI, Beaver Dam, WI 53916.

Serger Patchwork Projects by Kaye Wood (4949 Rau Rd, West Branch, MI 48661), 1986--free information on this and other publications.

Sewing With Sergers, The Complete Handbook for Overlock Sewing by Gail Brown and Pati Palmer,

Palmer/Pletsch Associates (PO Box 12046, Portland, OR 97212-0046), 1985, $7.95 postpaid; $9.95 spiral

The Successful Serging Handbook by Leonora Johnson and Sharon Hirscher, Tacony Corporation (1760 Gilsinn Lane, Fenton, MO 63026),1984.

Total Package for Teaching Overlock Sewing by Andrea Crisp and Diane Floyd (Rt 4, Box 196-CSI, Spokane, WA 99204), 1986, $20.00. Middle- and high-school teaching materials, including lesson plans, student worksheets, and overhead transparencies for an introductory serger course.

Sweaterknit Fabric Sources

Include your sweaterknit color, fiber, and weight preferences. Also ask about coordinating ribbed bands, collars, and ribbing by the yard.

Britex-by-Mail
146 Geary St
San Francisco, CA 94108
An amazing selection of spendy but scrumptious sweaterings. Swatches, $4.00 and a business-sized SASE.

G Street Fabrics
11854 Rockville Place
Rockville, MD 20852
Top quality sweaterings. Specialized swatching service, $2.00 and a business-sized SASE.

Golden Needles
209 East State, Box 208
Cherry Valley, IL 61016
Custom knit sweater yardage, bodies, and ribbing; specialty is border design that camouflages wearer's name in the repeat. Write for yarn color samples and prices.

Thrifty Needle
3232 Collins St
Philadelphia, PA 19134
Moderately priced acrylic, cotton, and wool sweater bodies and ribbing. Swatches and prices, $2; business SASE.

Specialty Pattern Companies

Burda Patterns
PO Box 2517
Smyrna, GA 30081
European styling and construction methods.

Great Fit Patterns
221 SE 197th Ave
Portland, OR 97233
Women's sizes 38-60.

Kwik Sew Pattern Co
3000 Washington Ave North
Minneapolis, MN 55411
Classic styles for knits and wovens.

Prime Moves
PO Box 3092
Gresham, OR 97030
Leotards and tights.

Stretch and Sew Patterns
PO Box 185
Eugene, OR 97440
Knit specialist, with styles for wovens too.

Recommended Sewing Publications

McCall's Patterns Magazine
230 Park Ave
New York, NY 10169

Needlecraft for Today
16th Floor, 1350 Ave of Americas
New York, NY 10019

Sew It Seams
PO Box 2698
Kirkland, WA 98083

Sew News
PO Box 1790
Peoria, IL 61656

Threads
PO Box 355
Newtown, CT 06470

Treadleart
25834 Narbonne Ave, Ste 1
Lomita, CA 90717

Vogue Patterns Magazine
161 Sixth Ave
New York, NY 10013

Index

ABOUT THE AUTHORS

Gail Brown

Sue Green

Pati Palmer

Gail Brown, a University of Washington Home Economics graduate, took her Clothing and Textiles degree to New York where she became marketing director for a fabric company. She has also been Communications Director for Stretch and Sew and has appeared on television including ABC/Hearst Daytime Series and AM Northwest. Her books include: *Sewing With Sergers, Sew A Beautiful Wedding, Sensational Silk,* the *Instant Interiors* home decorating series, and *The Super Sweater Idea Book.*

Gail's by-line appears regularly in *Sew News, Needle and Thread, Needlecraft for Today,* and *McCall's Patterns* magazine. She also consults for the *Fabrics by Lineweaver* mail-order catalog.

Pati Palmer owns her own publishing company, designs "Personalized Instruction" patterns for the McCall Pattern Co., and speaks to audiences throughout the U.S. and Canada sharing her extensive knowledge. In her career she has worked as an educational representative for the Armo Company, as Corporate Home Economist for an Oregon department store, and as a notions buyer. She is a Home Economics graduate in Clothing and Textiles from Oregon State University and was recently selected Oregon Home Economist of the Year. She is currently Vice Chairman of the Clothing and Textiles section of the American Home Economics Association and National Public Relations Chairman for Home Economists in Business. Pati writes for *Sew News* and *McCall's Patterns* magazines. She has co-authored *Mother Pletsch's Painless Sewing* (newly revised); *Pants for Any Body; Sewing Skinner® Ultrasuede® Fabric; Easy, Easier, Easiest Tailoring;* and *Sewing With Sergers.* Pati and Gail have both appeared on the Sewing by Satellite national teleconference.

Sue Green has been the leading serger expert in the United States for ten years. She entertains audiences with her light-hearted approach to this technical subject, not to mention that she can single-handedly take apart and reassemble any serger!! As former sewing machine and serger sales manager for a large fabric store chain, Sue was responsible for designing "how-to" lesson programs. As National Education Coordinator for one of the largest serger importers, she traveled the country conducting dealer training and consumer programs. She also developed serger workbooks and revised manuals. Sue writes for *Sew News, Sew-It-Seams* and *McCall's Patterns* magazine. She currently manages the four-day Palmer/Pletsch Serger Workshops held in Portland, Oregon.

We've repeated the instructions here for starting and ending threads so you can tear this page out and post it by your serger.

- **At the beginning of a seam**

1. Stitch one stitch into fabric edge.

2. **Then** lift presser foot and bring chain to front.

3. Pull on chain to make it narrow. Place on seam allowance and serge over it.

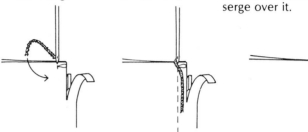

- **At the end of a seam**

1. Serge one stitch off the edge of the fabric. Gently slip the chain off stitch finger (pulling a slight amount of slack above needle will make this easier — see page 47). Raise presser foot. Flip fabric over and to the front of the presser foot.

2. Lower the presser foot and stitch 1"-2" over last few stitches. Be careful not to cut into the stitches already sewn. Chain off and trim the chain.

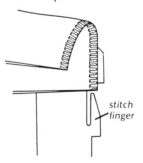

stitch finger

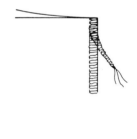

NEWS FLASH!!

The day we went to press on *Creative Serging Illustrated,* we learned a better way to remove threads. This method comes from Gale Grigg Hazen, author of *Sew Sane* ($14.45 postpaid from PO Box 4762-CSI, San Jose, CA 95150). As a child, Gale's job in her grandparents' upholstery shop was to remove serging threads.

Cut off the beginning chain even with the fabric. Separate the ending chain into individual threads. Grasp the needle thread(s) in your right hand and gently gather the fabric along the thread(s). When the needle thread(s) slide out of the fabric, the looper threads will pull out easily.